America's Race Problem

A Practical Guide to Understanding Race in America

Paul R. Lehman

UNIVERSITY PRESS OF AMERICA,® INC.
Lanham • Boulder • New York • Toronto • Plymouth, UK

Copyright © 2009 by
University Press of America,® Inc.
4501 Forbes Boulevard
Suite 200
Lanham, Maryland 20706
UPA Acquisitions Department (301) 459-3366

Estover Road
Plymouth PL6 7PY
United Kingdom

Library of Congress Control Number: 2009924646
ISBN: 978-0-7618-4572-0 (paperback : alk. paper)
eISBN: 978-0-7618-4573-7

Contents

Foreword

America is on the precipice of change. The opportunity for Americans to elect a woman or an African American as the Democratic Presidential Candidate for the first time in America's history represents a challenge never before available. America has the opportunity to show the world that its promise of liberty and freedom for all is not just a slogan, but also a reality. The problem America faces in meeting this challenge lies in the years of negative stereotypes associated with both women and African Americans that many Americans cannot easily dismiss.

If America chooses a woman as the presidential nominee, this act will set a precedent and signal to the world that a change in the American psyche is occurring. In essence, the negative stereotypes usually associated with women are on the decline. The same can be said for the selection of an African American nominee. The latter, however, would represent a dramatic change because it would involve the issue of race. From its beginning America has shown the world its feelings towards African Americans. What does this statement mean?

From the time the Africans were brought to America as slaves, their only significant value has been through the eyes of their enslavers, their market value. As far as their human value or self worth, that was perceived as negative. After slavery, the various social institutions created boundaries that kept the African Americans in check. The Jim Crow laws and violence, reinforced their negative image and injustice visited upon them. So, what does the slavery experience in America have to do with the presidential selection in 2008? The common theme that runs from slavery to today is race and the various implications it places on the society.

If a candidate were to be judged on character, intelligence, experience, and other qualities excluding race, then the challenge in selecting a woman or

African American would be simple. Given America's history regarding both women and African Americans, the problem becomes difficult. What lies in the way are the different perceptions of American society that conflict with one another. These perceptions involve how the world sees America; how America presents itself to the world; and how America sees itself.

Ask any visitor to America what he or she thinks of America and the immediate answer would be something to the effect that it is great, wonderful, marvelous, and probably a host of other complimentary adjectives. Ask how America treats its minorities, and one gets a different response. America is a diverse culture and a complex society so when someone from the outside looks in, he or she sees America from a perspective unique to their knowledge, culture and expectation. The BBC News recently did an Internet program on "message board" about America and solicited participation from around the world. The comments from the USA are excluded from the following until later. Also, the total number of responses is limited and offers here a sampling. The program's theme was "What do you think of America?"[1] America, we are told, is a country that was founded on freedom yet it was founded on mass slavery. America is a country where we are told free speech is valued yet when people speak out against the recent war they are vivified, fried or even attacked.

America is thought of as rich yet many millions of its citizens live way below the poverty line, and we simply don't care. America is a country where racism is alive and well. America is a country of basically decent people who allow themselves to believe in a fantasy worthy of Disney rather than change things for the better.

—Mike Peterson, Spain (Ex-USA)

America is still the leader of the western world and champion of democracy, which could have perished if not for the sacrifices made by the US. My regret is that the American people needed and deserved a more ethical administration to lead them in the aftermath of 9/11.

—Ken UK, England

I suppose that since America is such a young country, we shouldn't be surprised that they're now so gung-ho about making the kind of foreign policy mistakes that we in "Old Europe" were making 250 years ago.

—Stuart W, UK

I have been to the US and it is beautiful but the people are self-centered, highly opinionated morally limited and with Christian righteous, pro-Jewish values. It is scary how the country can become a dangerous weapon under a president with such a limited and narrow bandwidth.

—James, India

I'd like to see more comments from residents of Iraq, Libya, Afghanistan, Vietnam, Cambodia, Guatemala, El Salvador, Nicaragua, Panama, Croatia, Laos, Indonesia, and the other 30 or so countries the US has bombed since the end of the World War II. Any country the US cannot exploit or control it bombs back to the Stone Age.

—Mark, Ireland

The average American doesn't support critics or other ways of thinking. The US has nothing to do with the great tolerant democracy we used to know. Politicians there exploit their patriotism. They are totally misinformed but believe they are better informed than the rest of the world. And I think they have a special vision of their own history. By becoming ignorant Americans are becoming dangerous. The fear we have of them is nothing to do with jealousy.

—Luc, France

America as a country is representative of many western nations whose only knowledge of the rest of the world is TV. I don't blame'em but surely they are missing a lot. I wish they'd care to listen, travel and see the rest of the world.

—Lawrence gwakisa, Tanzania

America is a land of the brain washed public who can see no wrong in what is done in their name. If only the American people can look around and see that they need the world more then the world need them.

—Abdul, Egypt

The pictures of America we get from these comments are naturally mixed, but they do represent how the participants from various part of the world view America. Some of the comments were made in response to other comments made by some of the other participants. Each of these comments was selected in random order for geographical variety.

The next area of concern is how America presents itself to the world. The most obvious picture that America presents to the world is one of a freedom-loving society that respects the rights of each individual. The ideas of compassion and generosity for the downtrodden also fit into this image. The idea of America as a land of opportunity for all willing to work is a key incentive urging thousands of immigrants to her shores. We are frequently reminded of American sentiments expressed in the words of Emma Lazarus on the base of the statute of Liberty:

> "Give me your tired, your poor,
> Your huddled masses yearning to breathe free,
> The wretched refuse of your teeming shore,
> Send these, the homeless, tempest-tost to me,
> I lift my lamp beside the golden door![2]

The pictures we get and the emotions we feel every time we sing the national anthem or "God Bless America," "America the Beautiful," or a host of other patriotic songs represent genuine heart-felt love for America. These pictures and feelings are good and true. But they only represent one view of America. If we were to believe these images are the only true and valid pictures and feelings by Americans about America, we would be greatly mistaken. America is a complex society and as such has many sides from which it can be viewed. We just read a number of opinions expressed by people from different parts of the world about their feelings and perceptions of America. They all did not coincide with the pictures America has of itself. What do Americans, in general, think of America?

When we survey the preceding comments we find that most if not all of the participants mention some problems America face. One problem that is not addressed head-on is the problem of race. Why? One suggestion might be that the people involved in the program were not fully aware of the significance race has played in American history and life. After all, the Constitution does state that

> We, The People of The United States, in order to form a more perfect union, establish justice, insure domestic tranquillity, provide for the common defense, promote the general welfare, and secure the blessings of liberty to ourselves and our posterity, do ordain and establish this Constitution for the United States of America.[3]

Shortly after this statement, in Article I, section 2, paragraph 3, the framers wrote that

> Representatives and direct taxes shall be apportioned among the several States which may be included within this Union, according to their respective numbers, which shall be determined by adding to the whole number of free persons, including those bound to service for a term of years, and excluding Indians not taxed, three-fifths of all other persons.[4]

The reference to "three-fifths of all other persons" referred to the slaves who at this time were also called Negroes. History records the treatment of African Americans from the time of the Constitution to today; the views of America have been different for people treated differently. America's treatment of the African Americans in general represents a contradiction to what it professes. The following comments from "Studying American History," support this statement:

> I remember learning about American history as I grew up in the New York public school system. Much of it was European history. Of course, we had the one-day discussions, covered the requisite non-European topics such as Martin

Luther King Jr., Malcolm X, Geronimo, Sitting Bull, and a few others. But I remember learning more about England and our conflicted Presidents, whose practices usually ran contrary to their espoused values, than I did about the complex and multicultural history that is truly American history.

It wasn't until I attended college and enrolled in an African-American studies course that I became enlightened about a whole other side of American history that, at that time, was seldom taught in public schools. After learning about the contributions of African-Americans—their inventions and achievements (usually against all odds)—I remember feeling somewhat slighted by my public school education. I felt cheated, lied to, wronged. How many time had I encountered the arrogance of Whites who truly believed that African-Americans (or any other group for that matter) have never invented anything, never made any valuable contribution to our country.[5]

Some Americans believe that African Americans view America negatively because of the way they were treated during slavery. Many suggest that because slavery is in the past, African Americans should "get over it." What these Americans fail to understand is that Africans Americans do not hold a grudge against America about slavery and the treatment they received during that period of time, African Americans are more concerned with the treatment America has visited upon them since slavery. If the treatment had been fair and equitable then the various Civil Rights bills would have not been necessary.

This book presents the bases of American thought, language and practice on race from its early beginnings to today. The objective of the book is to help Americans recognize who they are, why they act the way they do, what they need to do to correct what problems they might have individually, and finally, what America needs to do to address its race problem.

NOTES

1. BBC NEWS Programmes: What do you think of America? http://newsvote.bbc .co.uk/mpapps/pagetools/print/news.bbc.co.uk/2hi/programmes/299724...4/7/2008.

2. Emma Lazarus, "New Colossus, *"Norton Anthology of American Literature 1820–1865, Sixth edition, 2003*, p. 2601.

3. Claudius O. Johnson & Associates, *American National Government, Sixth Edition, 1964*, p. 751.

4. Johnson, p. 751.

5. "Studying American History—not an issue of black or white, but both" http:// racerelations.about.com/od/ahistoricalviewofrace/a/americanhistory.htm.

Preface

America has a problem. America has had this problem since it became a nation. The problem is ethnic bigotry and its many ramifications. America knows about this problem, but refuses to address it realistically, that is, instead of America dealing directly with the problem, it has consistently chosen to deal with the effects of the problem. By constantly avoiding the cause of the problem, the problem, while seemingly going away, simply sits in waiting for another incident to bring it to the forefront. Americans like to think of themselves and their country as a symbol of democracy, and for all intent and purpose, it is, almost. What is and has been missing in America is a true and clear picture of its problem.

Dr. Martin Luther King, Jr. in many of his great speeches, but especially the 1963 speech in Washington, D.C. at the Lincoln Memorial, identified the problem for America, and suggested ways to address it. Many Americans today know King's speech as the " I Have A Dream" speech, and view it as inspirational, which it is to a degree, especially to European Americans. In reality, King's speech was a vigorous protest and indictment against America and its failure to deal justly with its problem. When we revisit the opening lines of his speech, we can see and hopefully, realize his deeply felt emotions concerning America's stubbornness and refusal to recognize and address its problem.

Dr. King, using the literary style of Lincoln's "Gettysburg Address" began his speech by making a reference to President Lincoln's Memorial as the setting and then to the "Emancipation Proclamation" as the primary focus attention He noted that one hundred years had passed since the issuance of that document whose purpose was to free the enslaved Africans. King noted that

Lincoln's proclamation was like a beacon of light and hope for the slaves who had not received justice in America.

Next, King reminded his listeners that the freedom expected by the Negro was still being denied them because society continues to hold them in bondage with segregation and discrimination one hundred years after Lincoln's proclamation. The Negro, according to King, finds himself poor and alone the in wealthiest and most productive nation in the world. What can be the reason for this ironic condition? In effect, King said that the Negro still is not accepted in his own country.

The primary point of King's speech was made clear when he created the metaphor of a check, symbolized by Lincoln's Emancipation Proclamation that has yet to be cashed. For him, the unsigned check meant that America has yet to honor its promise of life, liberty and the pursuit of happiness, i.e. full citizenship for all people. The time has arrived for America to honor its promise.

Dr. King's speech has been interpreted by many as a "dream" he has for America's future; however, the reference to his dreams come only after he has taken America to task for not honoring its promise, especially to African Americans. The speech, in essence, was a protest against American injustices, and a call to start practicing what it has been preaching about the guaranteed rights of the people found in the Constitution and Declaration of Independence.

King added that he believes the Negro people will not accept the idea that America has turned its back on justice, freedom and the opportunity for full participation in American life and society for all its citizens. The purpose of the march was to have America cash the check.

Today, America looks at itself and thinks that things are not so bad for the African American people. They have experienced upward mobility educationally, economically, politically, and socially. So what is the problem? As stated at the beginning of this work, America's problem is its willingness to give up its feelings about race.

In the following pages of this work, we will look at America's problem from a totally different perspective than those generally taken when discussing the subject of race. Looking at both the past and present should have given us a better understanding of the linkage and legacy of the problem. This book's organization will begin with an Introduction that lays out the thesis, followed by chapters on Race, Color, Normalcy, The Word 'Race,' Totem Pole, Challenges (which includes Perception, Language, and Behavior) and Considerations (The Race Box).

In each of the above sections information is presented to help explain and show how the problem has continued to manifest itself. A combination of information from both past and present is used. The objective of this effort is to underscore the need for change in America's status quo that was so skillfully presented by Dr. King back in 1963, and yet to be realized. Today, America can move pass the dream into the reality of its promise of unbiased freedom for all its citizens.

Acknowledgments

What goes without saying is that this work would not have been possible without the help of many people. First, thanks must go to God for allowing me to complete this work. Next I must give credit to my wife, Marion for all her efforts, encouragement, and understanding in making certain I had the time and space needed to work. A special thanks goes to my son, Christopher for his time and patience checking the manuscript. I wish to thank my immediate Lehman family, Yolanda, Jeffrey, Jenny, Imani and Erik for their encouragement and moral support, love and concern.

I also own a debt of gratitude to my siblings and their mates for their support and concern: Jim and Jo Lehman, Barbara and Billy Stubbs, and Lynda and Curtis Dick. Much in this book can be traced to some personal experiences as well as conversations dealing with some of the subject matter.

My extended family should also receive my thanks for their constant love and support in my efforts. These include Juanita and Bill Campbell, Morris and Mary Gonsoulin, Harry J. White, Jr., Keith and Drew Davidson, and my good friends Norman W.E. Satchell, Thomas and Alethia Carmans, and Donald Helberg. Others have been supportive as well, but are too numerous to name. I hope they understand how much they are appreciated.

Finally, I owe a special thanks to Michael Roselius for his technical assistance in putting this manuscript together. Without his help more time would have been required in organizing this material.

Introduction

America's race problem is like a man with a recurring headache who takes medicine to stop the pain. What he needs to do is find the cause of the headaches, and treat that cause. Otherwise, he will simply continue with the headaches followed by the medicine. Once the cause is recognized and treated, the headaches will not return. Unfortunately, America seems to enjoy just taking the medicine with each headache instead of dealing with the cause. At some point America has to stop and recognize the cause of its so-called race problems, and begin to address the cause.

America always seems to be in a quandary when some news item concerning race dominate the headlines. When the Don Imus[1] reference to the Rutgers Women's basketball term was brought to public scrutiny various factions of society became upset that such a thing could take place in America at this time in our social development. The idea that America has come a long way in "race relations" is a challenging statement because America has never gotten passed race. We delude ourselves into thinking that much progress has been made when in fact we have not moved far off dead center. When American society fails to be truthful about race, it teaches dishonesty to its children as well as shows them how hypocrisy works in real life.

Consider all the talk shows and town meetings and other community gatherings that attempted to get at the bottom of the race problem in America. Time after time different plans and strategies are created to deal with this problem head-on. After the dust settles, nothing really changes and cannot change because the real problem has yet to be addressed. What, one might ask, is the real problem? The real problem is race, and how we are made to relate to it. We constantly use terms whose meanings and histories we take for granted. By doing so, we make the same mistake, sometimes knowingly, over and over again. In essence, we make a mockery of our intelligence when we choose to use terms we know are incorrect, but provide privilege to one segment of society and discrimination against the other. Such is the case with the terms like *race, white*, and *black.*

A newspaper article, "Biology offers cancer clues," states "A new study gives a possible explanation for why breast cancer is more deadly in black women."[2] The article did not mention if the white and black women in the study were Americans. Should we assume that they are? Did the colors black and white mean black race and white race or did they mean that women with those skin complexions were the objects of the study? Without that information, the research study is meaningless. If white and black are used as colors, then all women fitting those descriptions should be alerted to the research findings. If the black and white colors are means to signify persons of European American and African American descent, then the study is still nebulas because all women of European descent are not the color white and all women of African American descent or not the color black.

As a society we find ourselves in a quandary by using terms that are based on false premises, words that say one thing but can mean a variety of other things. Of all people, scientists should know the difference between a color and an ethnic or cultural identity. America is too diverse a society/nation to continue using the terms black and white as catch words for so-called races. Who or what in the article defines the colors black and white? Certainly, the scientists did not. They simply assumed that the terms were fully acceptable and understood by all so, were appropriate for use in their scientific study. The fear of being politically correct should not come into play when the use of appropriate terms will render any conclusion more accurate and precise.

The article further states, "The study is the largest yet to link a biological factor to the racial disparity, which also has been blamed on black women getting fewer mammograms and less aggressive treatment."[3] The suggestion is that race is a factor in who get breast cancer. Since no race has been defined, only suggested by the use of the colors black and white, should the reader assume that race is a certainty? Eighty percent has been used as a relative acceptable number for a total of the world's people of color. Twenty percent represents the remainder. Does ethnic identity come into play regarding color or should one simply rely on color as the determinant of race?

The article leaves no doubt about the certainty of race playing the primary role in this study when it states that "'This put biology more to the forefront,' said Dr. Julie Gralow, a cancer specialist at the University of Washington School of Medicine familiar with the work. 'It's not just access to care, access treatment and other factors that have been implicated in the past.'"[4] Does the findings of this study prove conclusively that America has two races, one black and one white and that the women of the black race should be aware of their likelihood to contract cancer? Should dark complexioned women (black) coming to America from other countries and cultures also be concerned about this study?

The concern of this article and the study is not to belittle or ridicule it, but to point out the lack of accuracy in dispensing information based on false premises, and inadequate language, namely, in the use of the term *race*. The human race is diverse, so differences will certainly exist among peoples; however, we should not continue to promote the myth of races based on those differences. If the study focused on African American women and European American women, then the study should state that. The study should also define the study subjects in specific terms rather than general utility terms. For the study to do less, would simply be a waste of time for all concerned, because the result could not be validated.

When the subject of race is discussed, we seem to accept a definition that is very elusive except when it comes to mankind, the human race. Are some humans of a race different from *Homo sapiens?* We seem to think so if our language is any indication of what goes on in our minds. Although religion, science, both natural and social, tells us that we are all of one blood, we, as a society, have never been able to fully accept that fact. We constantly want to separate ourselves from others by using terms that are convenient, but incorrect. One term in particular is race. Why do we choose to hold on to this term when we know it to be inaccurate when discussions of cultural and ethnic identities are concerned? A value is placed on the use of that term. The value can be either positive or negative.

Another term used in association with race is *color*. Color terms represent one of the primary ways we attempt to distinguish ourselves from others. The problem is not the color, but what the color represents. As a society we have come to accept some colors as symbols of factual assessments regarding human beings. We judge character, behavior, morals, and a host of other things on the basis of color. Rarely do we challenge our social conception and perception of color; we choose to ignore it because by doing so we relieve ourselves of dealing rationally with the facts belying our use of color.

Although society uses a variety of colors when distinguishing one cultural or ethnic person from another, the two basic colors used in the Western World and in particular, America, are white and black. These two colors are used to separate large segments of society by associating positive and negative value with each color. Thereby making one color privileged and the other not privileged. Because of this phenomenon, American society cannot deal rationally with any problems of race. Common sense tells us that if the premise of a problem is false, the conclusion has to be false also. America must correct the premise before it can deal rationally with solving the problem.

In order to fully understand the problem and how society must address it if a solution is to be forthcoming; we must look first at how the problems of *race* and *color* came to be the stumbling blocks they are presently.

NOTES

1. Don Imus was a national television and radio talk personality who made some ethnic sensitive comments about the Rutgers University Girls Basketball team in 2007.

2. "Biology offers cancer clues," *The Oklahoman*, p. 4A.

3. 'Biology . . ." p. 4A.

4. "Biology . . ." p. 4A.

Chapter One

Race

To European Americans when the word race is used, the last image that comes to mind is the European American. The reason for this is European Americans do not consider themselves as a *race* of people, they consider themselves to be just simply people, normal people. All non-European people are considered members of a *race*. Why? because their perceptions of people have been changed over the years. History records the use of the term race by the English; it was used to separate themselves from some of their neighbors. Jacques Barzan, in his work, *From Dawn to Decadence*[1] says of this concern that

> . . . the idea of different 'races' replaced that of a single, common lineage. The bearing of this shift is clear: it parallels the end of empire and the rise of nations. Race unites and separates: We and They. Thus the English in the 16C began to nurse the fetish of Anglo-Saxonism, which unites them with the Germanic and separates them from the Roman past.[2])

Barzan does not mention color as a factor in the English determining the We versus the They. However, discernment was made to view their neighbors differently. Barzan continues:

> From the changed outlook a new group of words came into prominence: not only German, Saxon, and Angle, but also Jute and Dane, Gaul, Celt, and Frank, Norman, Lombard, and Goth. . . . The conviction moreover grew that the character of a people is inborn and unchangeable. If their traits appear odd or hateful, the theory of race justifies perpetual enmity. We thus arrive at some of the familiar prejudices and hostilities of our time. 'Race' added the secular idea of inborn differences to the theological one of infidel and Christian.[3]

Americans today know from scientific research projects like work on human DNA, and Stephen Oppenheimer's study of mankind, that the human race is simply one race. The world is not populated with groups of races. We know that human kind represents many cultural and ethnic differences, but only one race. Yet, we still behave and speak as if many races of human exist today. The suggestion that many races exist is just that, a suggestion or rather a myth. Many "nations" exist because of culture, geography, and ethnic differences, but "nations" are still part of the human family. Barzan comments on this fact from an historical perspective:

> What is false in this dogma is the belief that a nation is a race, a group sharing a common biological descent. Equating nation with race defies the most elementary knowledge of history. From time immemorial, Europe and America have been playgrounds of miscegenation. Celts, Picts, Iberians, Hittites, Berbers, Goths . . . and a host of lesser tribes once thought distinct mingled in and around the Roman Empire, a vast mongrel population. The Celt swept from Britain to Asia Minor; the Scots came from Ireland, Germanic tribes covered the Occident, Arabs and North Africans held southern part of it-and so on. Later, the conglomerates called nations mingled likewise through voluntary migration, exile, and the violent or willing crossbreeding of wars fought by multinational mercenary armies. Napoleon's troops at the last were drawn from all Europe.[4]

The term race as well as its usage in American society has long been questioned as well as challenged. In 1942, Ashley Montague, working with a group of renowned scientists, suggested that the word *ethnic* and *ethnicity* be used instead of the word race. Later, in 1945, he stated in his book *Race, Science, and Humanity*[5] that:

> The conception of an "ethnic group" is quite different from that which is associated with the term "race." The phrase "ethnic group" represents a different way of looking at populations, an open, non-question-begging way, and a tentative, noncommittal, experimental way, based on the new understanding which the sciences of zoology, genetics, and anthropology have made possible. A term is discontinued, retired, but another is not merely substituted for it; rather a new conception of human population is introduced replacing the old one, which is now dropped, and a term or phrase suitable to this new conception is suggested. The old conception is not retained and a new name given to it, but a new conception is introduced under its own name. That is a very different thing from a mere change in names. It is important to be quite clear upon this point, for the new conception embraced in the phrase "ethnic group" renders the possibilities of development of "ethnic group prejudice" quite impossible, for as soon as the nature of this conception is understood it cancels the possibility of any such development. It is a noncontaminating neutral concept.[6]

The most recent findings concerning human beings and race can be observed in a selection offered on the Internet entitled *Journey of Mankind, The Peopling of the World*[7]. This production created and produced by The Bradshaw Foundation, in association with Stephen Oppenheimer,

> Presents a virtual global journey of modern man over the last 160,000 years. The map . . . show[s] for the first time the interaction of migration and climate over this period. We are the descendants of a few small groups of tropical Africans who united in the face of adversity, not only to the point of survival but to the development of a sophisticated social interaction and cultural expressed through many forms. Based on a synthesis of the mtDNA and Y chromosome evidence with archaeology, climatology, and fossil study, Stephen Oppenheimer has tracked the routes and timing of migration, placing it in context with ancient rock art around the world.

In spite of our extensive knowledge and understanding of the term *race,* we still continue to use it. One reason for this continued use might rest in the fact that the word has some inherent values. As the English suggested in their use of the term, one race is superior to another. Therefore, every time the term *race* is used, an undertone of superior and inferior is present. Because of the problems associated with this the word, Montague made the suggestion to discontinue using it and use *ethnic or ethnicity.*

Since the word "race" carries with it a sense of inferiority and superiority, how is each quality acquired? For the English, it was a matter of ancestry. They believed they were derived from the Germanic people, and that the Germans were inherently superior to all other European peoples. According to Hugh A. MacDougall, in his book, *Racial Myth in English History,*[8] two primary myths formed the basis of the English belief. The first of these primary myths suggested that the origins of the early inhabitants of Britain were located in Troy. The second primary myth suggested that the Teutonic or Anglo-Saxon origins of Englishmen claimed a higher degree of historicity. These two national myths served as the foundation of their belief which led to further development of additional supportive myths:

1. Germanic people, on account of their unmixed origins and Universal Civilizing mission, are inherently superior to all others, both in individual character and in their institutions.
2. The English are, in the main, of Germanic origin, and their history begins with the landing of Hengist and Horsa at Ebbsfield, Kent in 449.
3. The qualities which render English political and religious institutions the freest in the world are an inheritance from Germanic forefathers.

4. The English, better than any other Germanic people, represents the traditional genius of their ancestors and thereby carry a special burden of lead-
   ership in the world community.

With these myths as proof of superiority, little wonder the English attitude
dictated their personal behavior and treatment of their neighbors. However,
the attitude of superiority was not limited to the English. The majority of the
European countries saw themselves better than non-Europeans. Typical examples of European attitudes can be seen in the activities of their explorers
and adventurers. The attitude of superiority by Europeans was based on one
or more of the following: culture, crown, or religion. These areas were used
to discern the Europeans from other people and the two common symbols
used for that discernment were color and culture.

As noted earlier, the scientific community has generally accepted the term
ethnic or ethnicity in favor of using the term *race*. The use of these new terms
will not eliminate the presence of bigotry and biases, but will force the perception of differences to a different level. For example, if two brothers with
the same parents get into an argument and refer to each other as bastards, the
intended negative impact of that term will not affect them directly because of
their similarity. However, if a friend of the boys enters the argument and
refers to either of them as bastards, the dynamics change because the friend
is not of the same family as the boys, so the interpretation of the term by the
brothers will have a different impact on them.

In essence, the use of the terms *ethnic and ethnicity* removes the boundary
around the relationships of the brothers and the friend. If the brothers and the
friend refer to each other as *friend* no restriction or boundaries exist. The possibility for bias still exists, however, but on a different and higher level. For
example, if one of the brothers refers to the friend as his best friend, or very
best friend. The concern at this point is not the differences between the brothers and the friend, but the degree of closeness.

What the term *race* has historically done is separate and divide people
based on differences, and that difference is what the new terms address.

Race for America has been a convenient concept to use as the majority European American thought appropriate for maintaining and granting privileges.
As far as the courts were concerned, America had only two citizen races, one
white and one African American. This mind-set became quite apparent in
1922 and 1923 when two immigrants applied for naturalization and American
citizenship; they were Takao Ozawa, and Bhagat Singh Thind.[9]

In the case of Ozawa,[10] we learn that he was Japanese. In October 1914, he
applied to be admitted as a citizen of the United States to the United States

District Court of Hawaii. Although he had lived continuously for some 20 years, attending school in California, and doing all the things generally seen as being part of good citizenship, his petition was opposed. The reason given by the District Court of Hawaii for the opposition was that Ozawa, having been born in Japan and being of the Japanese race, was not eligible to naturalization under section 2169 of the law. This 2169 section of the law limits naturalization to "aliens being free white persons and to aliens of African nativity and to persons of African descent."[11] Since Ozawa was considered to be a member of the Japanese race, he was told that under the law, he could not become an American citizen.

The part of the law that raised the greatest challenge was the reference to "being free white." No definition of "white" was available but that presented little problem to the court. In its findings the court stated that:

> We have been furnished with elaborate briefs in which the meaning of the words 'white person' is discussed [260 U.S. 178, 197] with ability and at length, both from the standpoint of judicial decision and from that of the science of ethnology. It does not seem to us necessary, however, to follow counsel in their extensive researches in these fields. It is sufficient to note the fact that these decisions are, in substance, to the effect that the words import a racial and not an individual test, and with this conclusion, fortified as it is by reason and authority, we entirely agree. Manifestly the test afforded by the mere color of the skin of each individual is impracticable, as that differs greatly among persons of the same race, even among Anglo-Saxons, ranging by imperceptible gradations from the fair blond to the swarthy brunette, the latter being darker than many of the lighter hued persons of the brown or yellow races. Hence to adopt the color test alone would result in a confused overlapping of races and a gradual merging of one into the other, without any practical line of separation. Beginning with the decision of Circuit Judge Sawyer, in Re Ah Yup, 5 Sawy. 155, Fed. Cas. No. 104 (1878), the federal and state courts, in an almost unbroken line, have held that the words 'white person' were meant to indicate only a person of what is popularly known as the Caucasian race.[12]

The court next provides a number of cases that all underscore its finding and adds to the confusion of determining the question, what is a white person? The rationale for their answer in opposing Ozawa was that he is not Caucasian. They arrived at that conclusion based on the following:

> The determination that the words 'white person' are synonymous with the words 'a person of the Caucasian race' simplifies the problem, although it does not entirely dispose of it. Controversies have arisen and will no doubt arise again in respect of the proper classification of individuals in border line cases. The effect of the conclusion that the words 'white person' means a Caucasian is not to

establish a sharp line of demarcation between those who are entitled and those who are not entitled to naturalization, but rather a zone of more or less debatable ground outside of which, upon the one hand, are those clearly eligible, and outside of which, upon the other hand, are those clearly ineligible for citizenship. Individual cases falling within this zone must be determined as they arise from time to time by what this court has called, in another connection (Davidson v. New Orleans, 96 U.S. 97 , 104), 'the gradual process of judicial inclusion and exclusion.'

The appellant, in the case now under consideration, however, is clearly of a race which is not Caucasian and therefore belongs entirely outside the zone on the negative side. A large number of the federal and state courts have so decided and we find no reported case definitely to the contrary. These decisions are sustained by numerous scientific authorities, which we do not deem it necessary to review. We think these decisions are right and so hold. [13]

The next case involved Bhagat Singh Thind[14] who was a full blood Indian born in Punjab, India. He had been granted a certificate of citizenship from the District of Oregon, but the Naturalization Examiner for the U.S. Government raised an objection believing that Thind was not white. If we follow the reasoning of the court in the Ozawa case then the only thing Thind must prove to gain his citizenship is that he is Caucasian, right? Well, not so fast.

In the endeavor to ascertain the meaning of the statute we must not fail to keep in mind that it does not employ the word "Caucasian" but the words "white persons," and these are words of common speech and not of scientific origin. The word "Caucasian" not only was not employed in the law but was probably wholly unfamiliar to the original framers of the statute in 1790. When we employ it we do so as an aid to the ascertainment of the legislative intent and not as an invariable substitute for the statutory words. Indeed, as used in the science of ethnology, the connotation of the word is by no means clear and the use of it in its scientific sense as an equivalent for the words of the statute, other considerations aside, would simply mean the substitution of one perplexity for another. But in this country, during the last half century especially, the word by common usage has acquired a popular meaning, not clearly defined to be sure, but sufficiently so to enable us to say that its popular as distinguished from its scientific application is of appreciably narrower scope. It is in the popular sense of the word, therefore, that we employ it as an aid to the construction of the statute, for it would be obviously illogical to convert words of common speech used in a statute into words of scientific terminology when neither the latter nor the science for whose purposes they were coined was within the contemplation of the framers of the statute or of the people for whom it was framed. The words of the statute are to be interpreted in accordance with the understanding of the common man from whose vocabulary they were taken. . . .[15]

Thind showed to the court that not only was he of Caucasian ancestry but also a member of the "Aryan" race. Its reply was that the term Aryan " has to do with linguistic and not at all with physical characteristics, and it would seem reasonably clear that mere resemblance in language, indicating a common linguistic root buried in remotely ancient soil, is altogether inadequate to prove common racial origin."[16] The Court further concluded that:

> What we now hold is that the words "free white persons" are words of common speech, to be interpreted in accordance with the understanding of the common man, synonymous with the word "Caucasian" only as that word is popularly understood. As so understood and used, whatever may be the speculations of the ethnologist, it does not include the body of people to whom the appellee belongs. It is a matter of familiar observation and knowledge that the physical group characteristics of the Hindus render them readily distinguishable from the various groups of persons in this country commonly recognized as white. The children of English, French, German, Italian, Scandinavian, and other European parentage, quickly merge into the mass of our population and lose the distinctive hallmarks of their European origin.[17]

Of particular note is the fact that the same person, Justice George Sutherland,[18] wrote the Court's opinion in both cases. Be that as it may, the point regarding race or who could be considered "white" was simply who white people said was "white." Science, ancestry, law or any other means of discernment of a so-called race was useless to all but the whites.

NOTES

1. Jacques Barzan, *From Dawn to Decadence, 1500 to the Present,* 500 Years of Western Cultural Life, Harper Collins Publishers, 2004.

2. Barzan, p. 108.

3. Barzan, p. 108.

4. Barzan, p. 694.

5. Ashley Montegue, *Race, Science, and Humanity,* Van Nostrand, 1963.

6. Montegue, p. 69.

7. *Journey of Mankind, The Peopling of the World;* (http://www.bradshawfoundation.com/journey).

8. MacDougall, *Racial Myth in English HIstory.*

9. Takao Ozawa v. US, 260. 178 (1922). http//laws.findlaw.com/us/260/178.html.

10. Ozawa, p. 1.

11. Ozawa, p. 5.

12. Ozawa p. 5.

13. The Multiracial Activist—United States v. Thind, 261 U.S. 204 (1923). http://www.multiracial.com/government/thind.html.

14. Thind, p. 4.

15. historymatters, p. 3.

16. Thind, p. 3.

17. Thind, p. 3.

18. Associate Justice George Sutherland ruled on a number of important cases, including one on Minimum Wages, and The Jones Boys. The two cases involving the "white race" are seldom listed in his biography.

Chapter Two

Color

European adventurers and explorers made a monopoly of the color white as being a symbol of normality, Christianity, privilege, superiority. These symbols were necessary for the Europeans because it gave them an advantage over the non-European peoples who represented over eighty per cent of the world's population

When the European explorers and adventurers first ventured away from their geographical area, they discover that much of the people they came into contact were the same as they except for one consideration, their color. Since the people they came into contact with had not seen a person of fair complexion before, they assumed them to be alien or godlike. When Christopher Columbus first arrived in the West Indies, he and his men were greeted with great deference because the Tiano Indians had never before seen *white* men or tall ships. They assumed them to be gods. Columbus and his party brought with them gifts of diseases from Europe. These diseases had a deadly effect on the Indians as well as a welcomed advantage to Columbus and his men. The mystery of these Europeans to the Indians as well as the deference paid to them all came to a halt when Columbus sailed back to Spain. He left a company of men to oversee their interest. These men were treated like demigods until they started demanding company with the Indian women. When Columbus returned, he found all of his men had been killed.

The die had been cast, however. The Europeans knew that their color could be used as a symbol of superiority among non-European peoples because of the mystery surrounding them. They quickly used their superiority attitude by giving names to people, places, and things. Throughout early American history we find references to Europeans as *white,* or *Christian* and instances of their lack of respect or concern for the people they came into contact with except for what they could gain from the association. The color white represented cultural superiority, and Christianity; culture represented religious, and educational superiority; crown represented financial and military power. So, the skin color *white* became a powerful symbol in America. Only *whites* were considered normal human beings, all other peoples were inferior.

The color white worked well in America for a while. American slavery initially knew no color. Any able bodied person regardless of color could be and was enslaved; first, the Spanish enslaved the American Indians. Next, when the English arrived, they introduced Europeans as slaves and indentured servants. We are told that

> At least thirty thousand people convicted of crimes in England were transported to the colonies during the seventeenth and eighteenth centuries. Judges were empowered to make a choice: either sentencing individuals to death or sending them to the colonies. Protest by colonial agents led to the suspension of transportation from 1671 to 1717, but the widespread sense that England was threatened by a wave of crime in the early eighteenth century led to the resumption of the practice[1].

However, the supply of Indians and English convicts did not keep up with the demand, so the Africans were brought over to satisfy the demand. Since the supply of Africans seemed unlimited, the need for the Indian and European slaves diminished. However, with so many Europeans now experiencing financial growth, discernment between whites and non-whites had to be made. That discernment had to give the appearance of fairness to all whites, while making certain that boundaries of social class did not change. Change did occur, however, and the focus of the change settled on color and geography. The African was made black, Negro, colored, and a host of other inaccurate term employed as indicators of identity.

What America did with respect to color was to make the color *white* symbolize superiority, normalcy, privilege, correctness, standard values and Christian values. The only other color of concern was *black*. America made this color represent the opposite of *white*. Since the premise of all this activity was not based in fact, it was myth, false. However, when society conducted itself as if all those assumptions were correct, then the acceptance of them became a matter of routine. In addition, when the term race was added to the color white, the results was a mixture of a superior human being created by nature and/or God. The term race carries with it the idea of an inherent superior difference as a result of some biological or natural occurrence. Although this assumption is false, the belief in it guarantees the favored human beings all the benefits of it being true.

The American attitude of white superiority was communicated through every fabric of American society and underscored in many ways. Lynching was one extreme method of communicating white superiority and control as well as black inferiority and helplessness. Another method was the media. Early motion pictures, especially the very first, *Birth of A Nation,*[2] underscored the immense power of whiteness in America and the gross negative perceptions of the African Americans. Theme films like *Tarzan, King of the Apes*[3]*,* showed the European American, Tarzan, as king of the apes, but also king of all the Africans he encountered. Watching the films, one is led to assume that Tarzan is king of the apes, and the apes are smarter than the Africans. What makes Tarzan so smart? his white skin. Why does he select an ape for his companion rather than an African? Again, his selection must be based on his view that the ape is smarter than the African. We are also led to believe that this newcomer to the African jungle knows more about it than the native because, after all, apes raised him.

Primarily, the language, government, and law have demonstrated superiority of race and color in America. In order to acquire, maintain and control power one has to control the symbols. As children Americans are told the story of how America came to be America. After praising the European adventures and explorers and their contributions, the focus generally falls on the Europeans known as Pilgrims and Puritans.

The Pilgrims and Puritans came to America from England separately. The Pilgrims came in 1620; the Puritans came in 1630. Because of their similar religious beliefs, they quickly joined forces. Their leaders believed that people should not seek to rise above his or her social status acquired from birth. They incorporated their religious beliefs with their secular beliefs and created communities based on those perspectives. The leaders were well-educated men who were familiar with the Bible and English law. These two qualities lead them to keep records of their experiences and actions while governing their communities. The language use was English. Because the explorers had claimed the north and south coast of eastern America for the English Crown, the Crown gave permission for settlement of this land. Naturally, everything written and recorded was in English.

American society as we know it today is said to have started with the Pilgrims and Puritans. Since they controlled the language, they had the power to recognize and not recognize things favorable or unfavorable to them and their communities. For example, when Roger Williams voiced his ideas of democracy and religious freedoms to the leaders of the Puritan community in 1635, he was indicted for heresy and divisiveness, and then banished. No one with power equal to theirs was around to argue for Williams. Their language was the law.[4]

English was the language spoken in the colonies, and the English culture that informed the leaders helped to create the government. For the Puritans, God's law was the measure whereby all people would be judged. However, only the leaders would do the judging. They believed that God gave to the leaders the "right reason" necessary to make all decisions concerning the governance of the society. The government was constructed to give the power to the leaders who believed that they acquired their positions through the grace of God. Therefore, anyone who disagreed with them also disagreed with the will of God. Now, that is power.

Another area of control and power was situated in the laws. The language was English, and initially the government was based on aspects of the Bible, English government and culture, and the laws were created to reflect those influences. After the war for independence, the government and the laws changed, the language remained the same. However, the one thing that did not change was the value of being of the white race. Superiority was grounded in one being European (white) and maintained and promoted by the law.

The most important laws for America are found in the Constitution. In the Constitution rest the evidence of ethnic prejudice sanctioned by the government. Article I, Section II, and paragraph 3 defined the slave as three-fifths a man. The term *slave* at this point in history meant any person of African heritage, free or not. Therefore, after the Constitution was ratified, all African Americans could and were seen legally as less than human being. Being considered less than human freed the European Americans and others of guilt in their treatment of the African and African Americans. Of course every state created laws to control every aspect of the slaves lives. Even the church played a significant role in this control.[5]

In one of his letters from *Letters from an American Farmer,*[6] Crevecoeur notes the following:

> A clergyman settled a few years ago at George Town, and feeling as I do now, warmly recommended to the planters, from the pulpit, a relaxation of severity; he introduced the benignity of Christianity and pathetically made use of the admirable precepts of that system to melt the hearts of his congregation into a greater degree of compassion toward their slaves than has been hitherto customary." Sir," said one of his hearers, "we pay you a genteel salary to read to us the prayers of the liturgy and to explain to us such parts of the Gospel as the rule of the church directs, but we do not want you to teach us what we are to do with our blacks." The clergyman found it prudent to withhold any farther admonition.[7]

The influence of the church on American law regarding the treatment of fellow human beings continues today as it did back before and after the Civil War. The church, even after the Civil war when law changes the treatment of

African Americans; the positive value of being European American remained the same as did the lack of value for being African American. In 1850, the northern Baptists church experience a great change that caused a split that resulted in the creation of the Southern Baptist Church. In celebrating their existence in 1995, the church issued these comments in an article from the *Daily Oklahoman*:[8]

> . . . the nation's largest non-Catholic denomination will observe their 150th anniversary by attempting to make amends for harm done since the group was born out of a split with northern Baptist over southern approval of slavery.
>
> "There's no question that the issue of slavery was part of our beginning 150 years ago," said the Rev. Anthony Jordan, . . ." . . . that's not what we stand for."

Conversations concerning the church's apology for its stand on racism followed nationwide. Some questioned the sincerity of the apology since the church had not supported a single civic rights bill throughout its existence. Although the Southern Baptist Convention made a public apology, their church was not the only one to practice discrimination. Other protestant religions simply did not publicize their bias beliefs and practices. Today in America, the church, with all its influence, is still the most segregated social institution in society. No doubt exist that the church's influences had a direct impact on the laws.

Since the Constitution gave permission for perceiving the Negroes as less than human, to act on those beliefs was not viewed as unethical, immoral, or criminal. The Five Civilized Tribes during the removal from their lands made certain to take their African, African American, Indian slaves with them. The reason for the title "Civilized" in reference to these tribes was due to the fact that the tribes were encouraged to pattern their lifestyle after that of the European Americans. In a work entitled *The Seminole Freedmen*,[9] the author, Kevin Mulroy, states that:

> During the antebellum period, as Native customs went into decline due to both internal and external pressures, slaveholding elites composed of wealthy intermarried whites and their mixed-race offspring emerged among the Cherokees, Creeks, Choctaws, and Chickasaws. Those elites assumed positions of economic, social, political, and cultural leadership and came to direct tribal policy regarding Indian-black relations. That highly acculturated plantocracy instigated the adoption of capitalist economies, democratic elections, constitutional governments, Christianity, school-based education, written laws and law enforcement agencies, institutional slavery, and severe black codes.[10]

The fifth tribe, the Seminoles, we are told, had "the lowest rate of white intermarriage and were the least acculturated of the Five Tribes.[11] In essence,

while the Indians were being driven off of their lands and being treated unfairly, they made certain to hold on to their valuable property, their slaves and
to treat them more poorly than their European counterparts.

Laws concerning *race* in America from the beginning of slavery until today always favor the European American. In America, white is always right.
But even more significant is the fact that every time the term is used it helps
to divide the population whether that is the intent or not. Take, for example,
the 1964 Civil Rights Law in which two sections, numbers 201 and 202, con-
tain the phrase "on the ground of race, color, religion or national origin." Although the law was intended to create better social conditions and opportunities for African Americans who had been deprived for many years, the terms
race and *color* does nothing to change the attitude or ideas of superiority by
the majority society. In essence, the law seems to underscore the separateness
of people of a so-called race and color from the normal European American.

In 1968, the Kerner Commission Report, actually the *US RIOT COMMIS-
SION REPORT,*[12] *(the New York Time)* a national response to the Watts Riot,
and general civil unrest in America expressed via riots in a number of cities,
stated what America had known all along, but had never admitted until this
report:

> This is our basic conclusion: Our nation is moving toward two societies, one
> black, one white—separate and unequal.
>
> Reaction to last summer's disorders has quickened the movement and deep-
> ened the division. Discrimination and segregation have long permeated much of
> American life; they now threaten the future of every American.
>
> This deepening racial division is not inevitable. The movement apart can be
> reversed. Choice is still possible. Our principal task is to define that choice and
> to press for a national solution.
>
> To pursue our present course will involve the continuing polarization of the
> American community and, ultimately, the destruction of basic democratic
> value.[13]

The report was like an elephant in the room—everyone knew what the reality of everyday life in America was like. The fact that the report stated that
America was a divided society was well known. The so-called new information was not new or earth shattering since America created each society
through its laws that gave privileges to one group and denied privileges to the
other. The report failed to deal with the real cause of the civil unrest because
they did not question their perceptions of race. They merely accepted the
myth of the existence of many races, rather than one human race. Preferring
to hold on to that myth keeps both groups from coming together as a society.
Understanding that stronghold goes back to the early years of nation building

as Pem Davidson Buck stated in the article "Constructing Race, Creating White Privilege[14]:

> To keep the racial categories separate, a 1691 law increased the punishment of European women who married African or Indian men; toward the end of the 1600s a white woman could be whipped or enslaved for marrying a Black. Eventually enslavement for white women was abolished because it transgressed the definition of slavery as black. The problem of what to do with white women's 'black' children was eventually partially solved by the control of white women's reproduction to prevent the existence of such children. The potentially "white" children of black women were defined out of existence; they were "black" and shifted from serving a thirty-year indenture to being slaves. To facilitate these reproductive distinctions and to discourage the intimacy that can lead to solidarity and revolt, laws were passed requiring separate quarters for black and white labors.[15]

From slavery through Reconstruction and beyond, discriminatory laws covered practically every aspect of the African American's lives. Civil rights laws were created with the intent of bringing some equity to the African Americans. Resistance to civil rights laws was common among lower class, working class, and middle class European Americans, especially in the South because those laws forced a change in the treatment of African Americans; however, the laws did not change the attitude of European Americans towards African Americans.

The idea of racial superiority in the European American will always be a factor in American society as long as a difference can be made between them and others. Anything that eliminates those differences creates problems of privilege, special treatment and identity being lost. Civil Rights laws focused on eliminating those differences hence, they were resisted. The laws did not actually remove the barriers blocking the African Americans' freedoms because the laws still underscored the separation between the two groups via the language used. The used of the word *race* in the laws simply underscored the existence of other so-called races.

NOTES

1. Heath Anthology of American Literature. Vol. 1 p. 268.
2. D.W. Griffith, *Birth of A Nation,* 1915. The first American film was the story of the Ku Klux Klan.
3. *Tarzan of the Apes* is a novel written by Edgar Rice Burroughs. The first in a series of books about the title character Tarzan.; it was first published in October,

1912. Tarzan was so popular that Burroughs continued the series into the 1940s with numerous sequels.

4. Norton Anthology of American Literature, 6th edition, Introduction.

5. Claudius O. Johnson & Associates, *American National Government,* 6th Edition, p. 751.

6. Crevecoeur, "Thoughts on Slavery, Norton, 6th edition, pp. 655–659.

7. Crevecoeur, p. 659.

8. "Baptists to look at Restructuring, Racism Issues," *The Daily Oklahoman,* June 19, 1989.

9. Kevin Mulroy, *The Seminole Freedmen,* The University of Oklahoma Press, 2007, p. 85.

10. Mulroy, p. 85.

11. Mulroy, p. 86.

12. The Kerner Commission Report, actually the US RIOT COMMISSION REPORT, 1968, *New York Times*.

13. Kerner, p. 1.

14. Pem Davidson Buck stated in the article "Constructing Race, Creating White Privilege," p. 33, in Paula S. Rothenberg, *Race, Class, And Gender In The United States*, 7th edition, Worth Publishers, 2007.

15. Rothenberg, p. 33.

Chapter Three

Normalcy

Although we cannot say if the concept of being normal was a conscious effort by the Europeans, the results are still that the only *normal* people in America are the Europeans. In reading American history generally, we find almost everywhere a reference is made to a people or persons of a different cultural identity, a qualifying term is used to discern the difference. In other words, all European people are usually identified as white or Christian, but all others are identified in terms that usually indicate an inferior status. An early example can be seen in this excerpt from the book *Foundations of Our Country:*

> One day in 1619 a Dutch vessel dropped anchor in the James River near Jamestown. The captain announced that he had come to trade. Part of his cargo consisted of twenty Negroes. The colonists gladly purchased the Negroes and put them to work on their plantations. Of course, the Africans were not bothered by the midday heat, and the tobacco planters preferred Negroes to white servants who could stand less work and ran away ofterner.[1]

Being normal in America means simply being European. Regardless of one's personal accomplishments, wealth, education, social position, the first qualification for being normal is being *white.* Normalcy for the European American is underscored in almost every aspect of daily life. The majority of media commercials depict European Americans using, doing, or being whatever is normal for America. When an ethnic Americans are depicted, the reactions is usually one of view them as an exception. Normalcy and privilege goes hand in hand in many instances. For example, most of the television shows including the cable channels usually show European Americans being normal. Occasionally, an ethnic American will be thrown into the setting for color (no pun intended). The ethnic American characters are generally seen as add-ons, not really a normal part of the setting.

Another way that normalcy is underscored in society is via product names. For example, when women shop for cosmetics, the color names of "natural," "nude," and "flesh" will all compliment the complexion of the European American primarily. Some exceptions exist today, but those exceptions are few. Interestingly enough, because of and other practices many European Americans believe and act like their normalcy based on privilege are natural and/or God-given rights, simply because they are *white.*

An interesting phenomenon in America is the fact that no one comes to America with a cultural or geographical identity of black or white. Europeans who come to America usually discover that it is to their benefit to identify himself or herself as white rather than Irish, German, Italian, or some other cultural identity. Those identities can create biases that would not come into play with being called simply, white. However, for the person of color coming to America, their cultural and geographical identity remains intact throughout their stay in America, because they know the stigma associated with being black in America and do not want to be associated with that negative image.

Take for example, many South American baseball players who have lived in America for ten to twenty years and still speak with their native tongue and American English only with an accent. Then, take a recent immigrant from Europe and see how long he or she retains their accent. The one possible exception for the European immigrant losing his or her accent would be an English speaking person. Americans value this accent because it reflects what they consider is normal. The French accent is considered by Americans to be sexy.

Because the Europeans controlled the language, government, and laws, they also controlled the values. For example, the standard of beauty for women in America is usually blond hair, blue eyes, and fair skin. That standard quickly eliminates a large percentage of the population who happen to be of color. Almost everything in America pertaining to everyday life is based on the values of European Americans. So, when the values one confronts everyday are familiar to ones self, the obvious conclusion is one of normalcy. Interestingly enough, America has always been a multicultural society, but the cultures that counted were European, France, Germany, Italy, Ireland, and generally, people from Northern, Eastern, Southern, and Middle Europe. The federal courts stated that:

> The words of familiar speech, which were used by the original framers of the law, were intended to include only the type of man whom they knew as white.

The immigration of that day was almost exclusively from the British Isles and Northwestern Europe, whence they and their forbears had come. When they extended the privilege of American citizenship to "any alien, being a free white person," it was these immigrants—bone of their bone and flesh of their flesh—and their kind whom they must have had affirmatively in mind.[2]

Just as the color white represented superiority in America, the color black represented inferiority. America's system of slavery changed the identity of the African from positive to negative. First, the name was changed from African to Negro, which means black. Once a people's identity was taken from them, their history and subsequently, their culture, and eventually, their language will follow. After a generation of being totally controlled by a master, the slave simply adopts whatever identity has been assigned to him or her. Once the cultural and geographical identity is taken, the new identity has value only in the new environment. For slaves, that identity was negative.

In 1905, the African American scholar, W.E.B. DuBois made the statement that the problem of the twentieth century would be the color line.[3] He was partially correct. The problem has never been the color per se, but what the color represents. As a society we have never gotten beyond the color.

While normalcy has its advantages, the most important advantage of being European (white) in America is *privilege.* We can study our history books from the days of the Puritans to today and still see and underscore the privilege associated with being white. Even in slavery, the Europeans, usually referred to as Christians, were given special treatment as stated in Thandeka's work, *Learning to be white*:

In 1705, masters were forbidden to 'whip a Christian white servant naked.' Nakedness was for brutes, the uncivil, the non-Christian. That same year, all property—horses, cattle, and hogs'—was confiscated from slaves and sold by the church wardens for the benefit of poor whites. By means of such acts, social historian Edmond Morgan argues, the tobacco planters and ruling elite of Virginia raised the legal status of lower—class white relative to that of Negroes and Indians, whether free, servant or slave.[4]

A recent example of the epitome of European American (white) privilege can be seen in a newspaper article from *The Oklahoman* in 2003. The article written by Leonard Pitts Jr.,[5] describes a European American woman's experience at the Abington Memorial Hospital in Abington, Pennsylvania, a suburb of Philadelphia:

. . . administrators at that hospital asked black staff members to stay out of the room of an unidentified woman who checked into the maternity ward in

September. This was at the request of the woman's husband who didn't want black doctors or nurses assisting in the delivery of his child.[6]

What would possess anyone to make such a silly request? Would not common sense dictate that the best-qualified professionals available would be called upon to assist?

The man's wishes were granted, according to Pitts. He goes on the state that

For the record, something very similar happened three years ago in Nashville. According to the Tennessee newspaper, a woman with a life-threatening hole in her heart asked surgeon Michael Petracek to exclude a black male member of his surgical team from the operating room. The doctor agreed.[7]

Although the professionals involved in both these incidents apologized later, they did honor the initial requests. Any ethnic American of color could not have made and been granted such a request. What we learn from these experiences is that America has not yet moved far from the attitudes of European American superiority and privilege prevalent in the sixteen and seventeen hundreds. What seems more puzzling than the request by the European man for his wife to receive special treatment is the willingness of the hospital staff to accommodate his wishes. American society is still evidently not quite sure of how it feels about race.

NOTES

1. J. R. Scoppa, *Foundations of Our Country,* Laidlaw Brothers, New York, 1930, p. 628.

2. "Not All Caucasians Are White: The Supreme Court Rejects Citizenship for Asian Indians, http://historymatters.gmu.edu/d/5076.html, p.3.

3. W. E. B. DuBois, *The Souls of Black Folk*, Bantham Books, 1989, p. 10.

4. Thandeka, *Learning to be white, Money, Race, and God in America,* Continuum, New York 1999, p. 43.

5. Leonard Pitts Jr., "The impersonal face of racism," *The Daily Oklahoman,* October 14, 2003, p. 6A.

6. Pitts, p. 6.

7. Pitts, p . 6.

Chapter Four

The Word 'Race'

Whenever the word race is used to represent identity it carries with it the quality of separateness or divisions because the suggestion of a race being superior or inferior is always present. Our use of the word 'race' and many of its derivatives are so irrational that they have become at times humorous. Take, for example, the Webster's New World Dictionary's inclusion of three traditional primary divisions of race as Caucasoid, Negroid, and Mongoloid. These categories have not withstood the test of scientific scrutiny because they were created by social scientists as suggestions, not scientific fact. In essence, the whole of the human race is divided into three basic groups of white, black, and shades other than those two. One scholar, Daniela Gioseffi, commented on the three racial designations and their lack of value:

> Since the turn of the century, social scientists, field anthropologists, biologists, and paleontologists have abandoned the useless classification of humankind into "Mongoloid, Negroid, Caucasoid," as if each stemmed from separate entities with individually different gestations. We know that we all crawled, fishy-tailed, from mud and we all stem from the same gene pool. The word race need be used only to specify the human race in all its manifest cultural diversity.[1]

Federal documents for years have listed on applications and forms, in general, two races, white or Caucasian (now European American), black or Negro (now African American). What happened to the Mongoloid? We never hear of someone referring to himself or herself as a Mongo or Mongoloid American. Lately, ethnic or cultural identities have been listed, but are still meaningless since the first two terms are still retained.

When the word *racial* is used, what does it mean? If mankind consists of one race, *Homo sapiens,* all the comments containing that term can refer to only one race. To associate physical, cultural, and geographical qualities of a people to a racial (meaning biological) character is simply irrational. Yet, we see it done all the time. At one point in American history scientists associated the size of the head and other parts of the body as being unique to a race of people. Many books have been written, and studies have been conducted to prove that humans are all different because of some geographical or physical feature or some other disposition attributed to nature. Scientists have shown that whatever those differences are, they are so minor compared to all the things that humans have in common.

Still, because America has not attacked the problem of race, the ignorance and confusion continues to manifest itself in a variety of ways. Hate groups who believe they are superior biologically to people of color, any color other than so-called white, seek to separate themselves from society. They try to promote their myth of superiority through club membership. One of the oldest such organization in America is the Ku Klux Klan. Other organizations with similar beliefs include The Aryan Nations, Skinheads . . . to name a few.

Nevertheless, in spite of the factual information available to these groups regarding their misconception of race, they still believe that the power and privilege they enjoy is rightfully theirs because of their "whiteness." The power and privilege derived from their philosophy of hate make it too difficult for them to relinquish.

Many Americans look at hate groups that use racial superiority as being of lower socioeconomic status, however, the genesis of these groups were clearly identified by Martin Luther King, Jr. writing in his work, *WHERE Do We Go From Here: Chaos or Community?*[2]

According to King, the general idea of the white supremacist is one of people who are poor, uneducated, and usually lacking proper social grace; people who would be sometimes refer to as "trailer-park" residence. That image, King suggests, is actually the opposite of the reality. The stereotyped white supremacist would not have been in a position to create, maintain, and promote the kinds of biased negative images of the African Americans. The reality, King notes, is that the genesis of these hate groups started with wealthy, educated, socially well-placed men. These men represented all areas of society from the businessman, to the lawyer, doctor, educator, minister, politician, and the lawman. With such a force promoting the theme of white supremacy, what could be the expectations of Negroes seeking justice?[3]

Just recently, a Nobel Prize winner, John Watson, was quoted in a statement to the effect that the entire continent of Africa is intellectually inferior to people of European descent. Patricia J. Williams[4] says of Watson that nent element that must be protected and defended at all cost. Will continued by stating that

> The next day's New York Times headline read: "RIOTERS HANG ANOTHER NEGRO. Mobs in Springfield, Ill., Defying 3,000 Soldiers, String Up Old and Innocent Victim"
>
> One hundred seventeen rioters were indicted. One was fined $25 for petty larceny; another, a teenager, was sent to a reformatory. Mrs. Hallam [the victim] later admitted that she invented the attack to explain some bruises inflicted by her boyfriend.[9]

One might think that since the above riot occurred so long ago, America has gone passed the time where race might create such a strong reaction or reaction. Unfortunately, such is not the case. Certainly we can hope that the reaction might not result in death and violence, but we also know that a lot of the sentiment regarding race is very much present.

NOTES

1. Daniela Gioseffi, *On Prejudice A Global Perspective,* Anchor Books, 1993, p. xiv.

2. Martin Luther King, Jr., *WHERE Do We Go From Here: Chaos or Community?* Hodder & Stoughton, 1968.

3. King, p. 74–75.

4. Patricia J. Williams, "False Prophets," *The Nation*, November 19, 2007. The reference is made concerning Nobel laureate James Watson who made contributions in the area of DNA research.

5. Williams, p. 6.

6. "Color, Controversy and DNA," A conversation between The Root Editor-in Chief Henry Louis Gates Jr. and Nobel laureate and DNA pioneer James Watson about race and genetics, Jewish intelligence, blacks and basketball and Watson's African roots. http://www.theroot.com/id/46667/output/print.

7. The Negro Holocaust: Lynching and Race Riots in the United States, 1880–1950, p.3 http://www.yale.edu/ynhti/curriculum/units/1979/2/79.02.04.xhtml.

8. "The Promise of possibility," George Will, *The Oklahoma*, 8-10-08, p. 5A.

9. "The Promise. . . ." p. 5A.

It seems pretty obvious that Watson has a social problem. Unfortunately, he is remarkably seductive in projecting his personal anxieties onto the population at large. He is dead wrong about the science, but just try arguing that to the average person. The blogosphere is ablaze with credulous exuberance at Inferiority Unmasked: racial difference is obvious but no one wants to talk about it. Racial sensitivity and political correctness are holding empiricism back. The worst part is how James Watson's position of authority substitutes for science. . . .

"Either he hasn't paid attention to his own field for the last decade or he's lying," says my colleague Dr. Robert Pollack, quietly and matter-of-factly. "I'm not sure which is worse."[5]

Sometimes words can be misinterpreted or used in a way that casts erroneous or misinformation relative to the speaker or writer. Because James Watson is a Nobel laureate and DNA pioneer, the statements attributed to him appear inconsistent with his scientific findings. Henry Louis Gates, Jr. in an interview with Watson asked about the statements attributed to him. In his response, Watson stated that:

One sentence was just taken out of my book. It was [that] we shouldn't expect that people in different parts of the world have equal intelligence, because we don't know that. [Some] people say that they should be the same. I think the answer is we don't know. . . . With the other two sentences, I talked to [the Times reporter] for eight hours. When I read the [quotes], I had no memory whatsoever of ever saying them. Because if I'd said anything like that, it was so inappropriate.[6]

In America, sometimes the word race does not have to be uttered in order for the meaning to come through. For example, the words negro and black are generally understood to precede race. Once either of these words are used in an uncomplimentary way involving European Americans, danger might exist for those living under either identity. The term "race riot" when used in America usually means a riot involving African Americans. Of interest concerning these race riots are the following fact:

1. In each of the race riots, with few exceptions, it was white people that sparked the incident by attacking Black people.
2. In the majority of the riots, some extraordinary social condition prevailed at the time of the riot: prewar social changes, wartime mobility, post-war adjustment, or economic depression.
3. The majority of the riots occurred during the hot summer months.
4. Rumor played an extremely important role in causing many riots. Rumors of some criminal activity by Blacks against whites perpetuated the actions of white mobs.

5. The police force, more than any other institution, was invariably involved as a precipitating cause or perpetuating factor in the riots. In almost every one of the riots, the police sided with the attackers, either by actually participating in, or by failing to quell the attack.
6. In almost every instance, the fighting occurred within the Black community.[7]

Some seven race riots occurring between 1880 and 1950 are considered most serious. They include Wilmington, N.C. (1898), Atlanta, Ga. (1906), Springfield, Ill. (1908), East St. Louis, Ill. (1917), Chicago, Ill. (1919), Tulsa, Ok. (1921) and Detroit, Mich. (1943).

George Will, *Washington Post* writer, recounts the incidents that led to the Springfield riot where a young European American woman was awakened during the night by the weight of a man's body on her. She reported that she had been raped by a black man. Once the newspaper got wind of the incident it went to work writing to inflame the majority citizens of the town. The police paraded black man after black man before her until she selected one as her attacker, one George Richardson. He was arrested and jailed, but a group of the local majority men wanted to lynch him. When the sheriff moved him to a jail in a nearby town, the men became angry and proceeded to initiate violence and destruction.

Will states that

> For the next six hours the rioters, fueled by liquor looted from the restaurant, sacked two black neighborhoods, setting fires and blocking fire wagons and cutting their hoses. Forty black homes were destroyed, as were 21 black and several Jewish businesses. Thousands of Springfield's blacks fled into the countryside; some never to return.
>
> After beating an elderly black man and a paralyzed black man, at 2 a.m. the mob seized a 56-year-old black barber from his home, beat him unconscious, hanged him from a tree and mutilated his body. Souvenir hunters carved away bits of the tree, which was entirely gone by the end of the day.
>
> The next night a mob of 500 brought a rope and proceeded to the home of a prominent and wealthy 84-year-old black man who, standing in front of his house, inquired, "Good evening, gentlemen. What can I do for you?" He was beaten, slashed with a razor, hanged from a tree too supple to bear his weight. He was alive when troops from the state militia reached him. He died that night.[8]

What caused all the violence, death and destruction? The answer is not that a male assaulted a female, a crime in itself, but that an African American male assaulted a European female. Race in and of itself was meaningless, but when negro, black, and /or white is introduced into the mix, value becomes a prominent element that must be protected and defended at all cost. Will continued by stating that

> The next day's New York Times headline read: "RIOTERS HANG ANOTHER NEGRO. Mobs in Springfield, Ill., Defying 3,000 Soldiers, String Up Old and Innocent Victim"
> One hundred seventeen rioters were indicted. One was fined $25 for petty larceny; another, a teenager, was sent to a reformatory. Mrs. Hallam [the victim] later admitted that she invented the attack to explain some bruises inflicted by her boyfriend.[9]

One might think that since the above riot occurred so long ago, America has gone passed the time where race might create such a strong reaction or reaction. Unfortunately, such is not the case. Certainly we can hope that the reaction might not result in death and violence, but we also know that a lot of the sentiment regarding race is very much present.

NOTES

1. Daniela Gioseffi, *On Prejudice A Global Perspective,* Anchor Books, 1993, p. xiv.

2. Martin Luther King, Jr., *WHERE Do We Go From Here: Chaos or Community?* Hodder & Stoughton, 1968.

3. King, p. 74–75.

4. Patricia J. Williams, "False Prophets," *The Nation*, November 19, 2007. The reference is made concerning Nobel laureate James Watson who made contributions in the area of DNA research.

5. Williams, p. 6.

6. "Color, Controversy and DNA," A conversation between The Root Editor-in Chief Henry Louis Gates Jr. and Nobel laureate and DNA pioneer James Watson about race and genetics, Jewish intelligence, blacks and basketball and Watson's African roots. http://www.theroot.com/id/46667/output/print.

7. The Negro Holocaust: Lynching and Race Riots in the United States, 1880–1950, p.3 http://www.yale.edu/ynhti/curriculum/units/1979/2/79.02.04.xhtml.

8. "The Promise of possibility," George Will, *The Oklahoma*, 8-10-08, p. 5A.

9. "The Promise. . . ." p. 5A.

Chapter Five

Totem Pole

Although some might find it hard to believe, a so-called racial totem pole still exists in America. This totem pole supposedly shows the value of human being in America. At the very top of the pole is the European American male with wealth and/ or power or both, next, is the female with similar qualities. Below the European female come the European males and females in general. Their socioeconomic status or the lack of the same will place them in the appropriate proximity to the top groups. After the European Americans on the totem pole come any ethnic American of wealth and power with the exception of African Americans. African Americans are to be at bottom of the pole regardless of their socioeconomic status. The reason for this position goes back to the beginning of American slavery and the negative value or lack of value attributed to the African. Their position at the bottom of the totem pole does not mean that those above the African Americans get a free pass. Concessions were made to poor European Americans based on their color as Pem Davidson Buck states:

> The initial construction of whiteness had been based on a material benefit for Whites: land, or the apparently realistic hope of land. By the 1830s and 1840s, most families identified by their European descent had had several generations of believing their whiteness was real. But its material benefit had faded. Many Whites were poor, selling their labor either as farm renters or as industrial workers, and they feared wage slavery, no longer certain they were much freer than slaves. But this time, to control unrest, the elite has no material benefits they were willing to part with. Nor were employers willing to raise wages. Instead, politicians and elites emphasized whiteness as a benefit in itself.[1]

What many non- elite European Americans failed to see, some still fail to see, is the manipulation of them throughout their existence by means of psychology. We learn from history how their minds were controlled:

> The work of particular white intellectuals, who underscored the already existing belief in white superiority and the worries about white slavery, was funded by elites and published in elite-owned printing houses. These intellectuals provided fodder for newspaper discussions, speeches, scientific analysis, novels, sermons, songs, and blackface minstrel shows in which white superiority was phrased as if whiteness in and of itself was naturally a benefit, despite its lack of material advantage. This sense of superiority allowed struggling northern Whites to look down their noses at free Blacks and recent immigrants, particularity the Irish. This version of whiteness was supposed to make up for their otherwise difficult situation, providing them with a "psychological wage" instead of cash—a bit like being employee of the month and given a special parking place instead of a raise.[2]

Since the European American set the standard for normality, ethnic Americans who try to act normal are often accused of "acting white." Actually, they are only trying to act normal, or under given circumstances, rational.

The totem pole philosophy does not exist only with the European Americans. Practically every ethnic group in America has its own sense or system of priority. The system is generally based on socioeconomic status similar to the European American, but not always. For some groups, another way of viewing the discernment of differences is know as class status. With class rankings, many elements besides socioeconomic status are taken into consideration including, but not limited to ancestry, family ties, and notoriety. In America the classes are identified as "working class," "middle class," "lower class," "upper class," and "ruling class." Although these classes actually exist in American society, few Americans will admit to membership in a class unless it is higher than their reality. The reason for this lack of wanting to be identified with a particular class is based on the common democratic idea of all people being equal. In an essay, "Media Magic Making Class Invisible,"[3] Gregory Mantsios says that

> The United States is the most highly stratified society in the industrialized world. Class distinctions operate in virtually every aspect of our lives, determining the nature of our work, the quality of our schooling, and the health and safety of our loved ones. Yet remarkably, we, as a nation, retain illusions about living in an egalitarian society. We maintain these illusions, in large part, because the media hides gross inequities from public view. In those instances when inequities are revealed, we are provided with messages that obscure the nature

of class realities and blame the victims of class-dominated society for their own plight.[4]

Mantsios maintains that the media controls the information available to the general public, and the information the public receives is manipulated.

> Those who own and direct the mass media are themselves part of the upper class, and neither they nor the ruling class in general have to conspire to manipulate public opinion. Their interest is in preserving the status quo, and their view of society as fair and equitable comes naturally to them. But their ideology dominates our society and justifies what is in reality a perverse social order—one that perpetuates unprecedented elite privilege and power on the one hand and widespread deprivation on the other.[5]

The primary reason for class distinctions within ethnic groups has to do with perceptions of human value and privilege. For example, during the early days of the Civil Rights movement in America, a phenomenon known as "white flight" occurred in many urban centers. The reason for the "white flight" was privilege in that many European Americans of "working class," "lower class, and "middle class" felt less valued when an ethnic American of color moved into their neighborhood or community. The European Americans usually moved to an area inhabited by European Americans only. In essence, the ethnic Americans were attempting to live on a social level equal to the European Americans. If that occurred, the privilege of being "white" would lose much of its value.

Ironically, when people of the "upper class" and "ruling class" find themselves living next to ethnic Americans, little is made of it. No European American has ever complained of living next to Oprah Winfrey or Tiger Woods because of their ethnicity. After all, socioeconomic status has some privilege in America in spite of ethnic identity.

Many terms have been coined that describe ethnic Americans who attempt to act rationally. Some of the terms include *Oreo,* meaning an African American who is black on the outside, but white on the inside. The term *Apple* has been used for American Indians, and the term *Banana* used Asian Americans. The point is that many Americans believe that to act normal or rational is to act white. Such is the power of white privilege in America.

Africans and African Americans were told and made to believe they were worthless in and of themselves. Their value was only in the worth placed on them by the whites. In fact, the value of being white was so important that even today only two whites, male and female, could produce a white off spring. No other male is the world can produce a white off spring. Being white even in parts was also valuable for the slave market. The more a slave looked like the master's race, the more money the master could get for that slave at market. Some slaves took to heart that the closer one looked like the master, the better those slaves or persons were closer to being a normal human being.

Today, that same sense of value exists among some very confused Americans who refer to themselves as *biracial,* meaning they are part of two distinct races. How can that be if only one race of human being exists? They would have to be part human and something else. The belief ties in with the old slave master's philosophy about the value of white in the market place. The slave masters coined terms to attract more money for their slaves of mixed blood. Terms like *mulatto, quadroon*, and *Octoroon* meant having one parent black and one white or a combination of the two valued in measurements of one half, one quarter, and one eighth, respectively. Although many states in their laws recognized the term "mulattoes," their treatment was the same as for slaves. After the Civil War, the same practice held true. DuBois in his work, *The Black Codes*, notes that Mississippi enacted the following law:

> That all freedmen, free Negroes, and mulattoes in this state over the age of eighteen years, found on the second Monday in January, 1866, or thereafter, with no lawful employment or business, or found unlawfully assembling themselves together, either in the day or night time, and all white persons so assembling with freedmen, free Negroes or mulattoes, or usually associating with freedmen, free Negroes or mulattoes on terms of equality, or living in adultery or fornication with a freedwoman, free Negro or mulatto, shall be deemed vagrants, and on conviction thereof shall be fined in the sum of not exceeding, in the case of a freemen, free Negro or mulatto, fifty dollars. . . .[6]

Many slaves were led to believe they were better than slaves of darker complexions, but the masters never saw them as nothing more than more money. Many African Americans not only bought into this myth, but also continued to promote and endorse it among themselves after slavery.

For the slave traders, however, the value of slaves was measured in dollars. Their traders gave slaves a variety of names:

> In March 1832, for instance, James Franklin wrote to [Rice] Ballard from Natchez. Eager for the next day sales to begin:" I shall open my fancy stock of Wool and Ivory early in the morning. The younger Franklin's words evoked a peddler opening a case to display cloth and carved knickknacks, although he referred to enslaved African Americans. His "wool" suggested common racist descriptions of their hair, and his "ivory" evoked both African origins and the teeth

that buyers inspected. Franklin described the enslaved as inanimate articles, stilled of life, and reduced to hair and teeth: "Wool and Ivory."

Slavemongers also referred incessantly to men, women, and children as "stock": James Franklin reported to Ballard after reaching Natchez in the fall of 1832 that "we arrived in this place . . . with all of our stock." Other references to their human merchandise underlined the deanimation inflicted in the traders' own minds. James, always a reliable font of offensive expressions, also wrote to Ballard in 1834, saying, "I suppose you are not buying any Cuffys right now." Later, his uncle also used the term, reporting, "The price of Cuffy comes on whether they have fallen or not they are very high through all the country." The singular term "Cuffy" standardized the human produce shipped from the Chesapeake, using a partitive term to imply that selling slaves was no different from selling "soup" or "lumber." The product was uniform: the main difference between one and thirty was one of the quantity of packages.[7]

All slaves were different to the traders only in the amount of money they were worth. The idea of being part white adding to personal character or intelligence was nowhere to be found among the traders:

> To be sure, Franklin and Ballard sought a mix of types of slaves. In November 1833, Isaac Franklin complained to Richmond that "[I] Could have sold as many more if we had of had the right kind, men from 8 to 900 dollars, field women large and likely from 6 to 650 dollars." He also reported "a Great demand for fancy maids[s]" as well as artisans and other skilled workers. Franklin also complained to Ballard about a recent shipment that did not meet standard size and age requirements: "yours and Armfields was the leanest invoice I have ever received. In fact your little slim assed girls and boys are intirely out of the way and cannot be sold for a profit." Each variety was identical within itself, measured and assigned a certain dollar value to correspond to the quantity of "Cuffy" [an African or African American person] that he or she contained.[8]

Even the term multiracial is a misnomer. All Americans are multiethnic. No so-called pure race of humans exists outside of the *Homo sapiens.* The idea of a black race is no longer viable nor is the thought of African Americans being born with identical genes that make them inferior to European Americans. In reality other than having some ancestry of African decent, the only common element that African Americans share is the biased and discriminatory treatment forced upon them an the subsequent legacy of the system of slavery. Race, in essence, has never been a factor in creating humans of inferior or superior character. Race has always been a creation of the European man's ego. In fact, today's scientists not only state that all life, as we know it began in Africa, but also that we are more alike than we are different according to DNA. As a matter of fact, international scientists who study the entire human genetic material conducted a study of DNA, known as The Human Genome Project. One of the results of this project according to one scientist is noted as follows:

> "The folk concept of race in America is so ingrained as being biologically based and scientific that it is difficult to make people see otherwise," said Sussman, a biological anthropologist. "We live on the one-drop racial division—if you have one drop of black or Native American blood, you are considered black or Native American, but that doesn't cover one's physical characteristics.
>
> "Templeton's paper," Sussman continued, "shows that if we were forced to divide people into groups using biological traits, we'd be in real trouble. Simple divisions are next to impossible to make scientifically, yet we have developed simplistic ways of dividing people socially."[9]

One of the more irrational uses of the word race comes from the word *racist*. If anyone bothers to look up the word *racist*, he or she will discover that a single human being cannot be a racist because the essence of that term's meaning depends on a group of people being thought of as inferior or superior to each other or others. That being the case, an individual can only be a representative of a racist people, but not a racist in isolation. The term *racist* is an adjective, and its use is usually in conjunction with a noun, a racist person. For example, an African American living in America cannot be a racist or a racist person because in order to be a racist, the people with which he or she identities must have the power to create, maintain and promote the superior difference. African Americans in America do not have and have never had that power. The opposite is true, however, for the European Americans.

As a society, we talk about race all the time and in every conceivable context, but who defines race? Ironically, when we are able to locate any early historical definition of race it usually comes from the constitution of a state. The State of Oklahoma, for example, defined race in its Constitution in Article XXIII, section 11, as follows:

> Wherever in this Constitution and laws of this state, the word or words, "colored" or "colored race," or "Negro" or "Negro race," are used, the same shall be construed to mean or apply to all persons of African descent. The term "white race" shall include all other persons.[10] (This law was repealed in 1978)

What we discover in this definition is the irony of all ironies, *race*, according to the law, is not about skin color or complexion at all, but about geography. The reference to African descent eliminates the necessity for color, so why create two races based on color?

One might think that being European American (white) entitles one to all the privileges enjoyed by all Europeans Americans. Not so. Just as the Angles discriminated against the Brits back in the 16th Century, today, European Americans separate themselves from each other on the basis of wealth, education, and social status. When an European American of upper or middle-class standing wants to distinguish himself or herself from an European American of low economic and educational standing, the latter is commonly referred to as "poor white trash," "trailer park trash," or "redneck." With few exceptions, ethnic Americans are in the minority as users of these terms because they are already discernable from the European American. In a democracy, the value of a human being should not be based on education, economic, and/or social status. The perception of having human value should be the same for all.

NOTES

1. Buck, p. 35.
2. Buck, p. 35.
3. "Media Magic Making Class Invisible," Gregory Mantsios, in Rothenberg's *Race* . . . p.182.
4. Mantsios, 184.
5. Mantsios, p. 185.
6. W.E.B. DuBois, "The Black Codes, p. 467, in Rothenberg's *Race*, 5th edition, 2000.
7. "Cuffy, Fancy Maids, and One-Eyed Men," Edward E. Baptist, *American Historical Review,* Vol. 106, Issue 5, Dec. 2001, p. 1916.
8. Baptist, p. 1633–1634.
9. "The Human Genome Project," Bruce H. Lipton, Http://www.money-health-relationships.com/humon-genome-project.html. p. 2.
10. James Shannon Buchanan & Edward Everett Dale, *A History of Oklahoma,* "The State of Oklahoma Constitution," Article XXIII, section 11, Row, Peterson, and Company, 1924.

Chapter Six

America's Slavery Legacy

America has long believed that it is the "shining light on the hill" with respect to justice and opportunity for all. Any comments to the contrary are usually placed in the unpatriotic or ungrateful category. In essence, some Americans do not see and/or do not want to see other sides of the American profile. That being the case, any problems America has that she does not acknowledge will remain problems. The central truth is that before America can began to deal honestly with its problem of race, it must first acknowledge the truth of its history—its bias against people of African American heritage—Negroes, coloreds, blacks, etc. . . . . That acknowledgement is its first major obstacle. No progress can be made in truth, if America does not recognize and accepts its actual history.

In America's "Pledge of Allegiance" the words "One nation under God with liberty and justice for all" remains the single most accepted idea of what America is as a society. Unfortunately, that concept of America is false. America has never been "One nation under God " except to those who refuse to acknowledge reality. Why? Race. What we know is that America's system of slavery was a dual system as well as a dual tragedy. For the European American, they were led to believe that they were inherently superior to African Americans. That belief did not change after the Civil War. As a matter of fact, that belief of superiority and privilege is the legacy created by slavery that still influences much of American life today. Simply stating the problem of race does not prove it existence or make it go away, however, if we look at a few of the significant documents and actions regarding America's story, the picture should become much clearer.

Many people look to Abraham Lincoln as the great emancipator because he issued the "Emancipation Proclamation." Contrary to popular belief, that document did not free the slaves, only some slaves. The states that were not in rebellion with the United States could keep their slaves and their system. Fearing that his actions would be interpreted as a war measure, Lincoln helped push through congress, the 13th and 14th Amendment. If we look at these Amendments we discover that America had not included all people as equally part of society. AMENDMENT XIII, Section 1, reads: "Neither slavery nor involuntary servitude, except as a punishment for crime whereof the party shall have been duly convicted, shall exist within the United States or any place subject to their jurisdiction." Section 2, states that "Congress shall have the power to enforce this article by appropriate legislation."[1]

Slavery in America was not ended legally until these two Amendments were passed. The mere fact that they had to be passed showed that American society did not embody the "One Nation" concept. The passing of these two articles did not insure that all Americans would enjoy the "blessing of liberty and justice" to which they were entitled. The social institution made certain that would not happen.

Several pieces of legislation passed at the national level underscore the legacy and attempts to dislodge it from its place of importance in society. After the Civil War and Reconstruction, legal, social, religious, political, and cultural restrictions created, maintained, and promoted by European Americans kept the African Americans from full participation in American life. The problems of these restrictions generally known as "Jim Crow" activities came to a head in 1954 when a civil case came to the Supreme Court. The case was *Brown v. Topeka Board of Education.* The Chief Justice, Earl Warren said: "In the field of public education the doctrine of 'separate but equal' has no place."[2] Justice Warren continued by stating that separating African American children from European American children would have a lasting negative affect on them. He maintained that by separating them "from others of similar age and qualifications solely because of their race generates a feeling of inferiority as to their status in the community that may affect their hearts and minds in a way unlikely ever to be undone."[3]

Any pretext to America being "One nation" prior to the *Brown* decision lost its value once the Court's implementation went into effect. This decision had an impact on all America, not just African Americans. European Americans felt their status and privileges were under attack. So, to counter the effects of the Court's decision, they began to flee the urban areas. The movement of the European Americans from the cities became known as "white flight." Many of the suburban areas where the European Americans fled to were successful in achieving two major actions—continuing segregation based on so-called race, and creating economic difficulties for the cities being vacated.

Prior to the *Brown v. Topeka Board of Education* America was well within the law to segregate itself. In part this legal authority was made possible by the Court's decision in *Plessy v. Ferguson* which made "separate but equal" the law of the land; however, the *Brown* decision overruled this "separate but equal" law and created an atmosphere of hatred and hostility against African Americans. The primary reason for this hatred and hostility was the fact that the courts were taking away the privileges of being European American (white), which was thought to be irrevocable since superiority was viewed as inherent. How could America go back on its word and have African Americans and European Americans viewed as equals?

Congress passed several "civil rights" acts since the end of the Civil War:

Between 1865 and 1875 Congress enacted six or seven rather comprehensive civil rights statutes designed primarily further to secure the Negro (although the race was not named) in the rights he was supposed to have acquired under the Thirteenth, Fourteenth, and Fifteenth Amendments. Of these statutes only a few provisions survive in the present U.S. Code. Sections of the Code (Title 18, sec. 1581-88) define slavery and peonage and specify the punishment for individuals holding others in those conditions. A section (Title 18, sec. 241) makes it criminal for two or more persons to "conspire to injure, oppress, threaten, or intimidate any citizen in the free exercise or enjoyment of any right or privilege secured to him by the Constitution or laws of the United States."; or for "two or more persons to go in disguise on the highway, or on the premises of another [aimed at the Ku Klux Klan], with intent to prevent or hinder his free exercise or enjoyment of any right or privilege so secured." And another section (Title 18, sec. 242) penalizes anyone who, "under color of any law . . . willfully subjects any inhabitant...to the deprivation of any rights, privileges, or immunities secured or protected by the Constitution or laws of the United States. . . ."[4]

Some European Americans might want to excuse society for the way it discriminated against people of African heritage since not much time had passed since slavery ended. However, the fact those laws were necessary to force society's behavior regarding the treatment of African Americans underscore the fact that they had not been treated fairly. In addition, Congress did not pass any additional civil rights legislation after the above until 1957.

The Civil Rights Act of 1957 coming on the heels of the *Brown* decision was important in that it spoke to the fact that African Americans had previously been denied the vote by the majority society through violence and intimidation. The law prohibited any action that would prevent persons from voting in federal elections. The Attorney General was empowered to bring suit when a person was deprived of his or her voting privilege. Without the vote, African Americans could not participate or influence legislation concerning themselves and others. Of further importance regarding this Act were the creation of a Civil Rights Commission, and the establishment of a Civil Rights Division in the Department of Justice.

Many majority Americans joined in the fight for civil rights and fair justice for African Americans in particular, and all Americans in general. They realized from the beginning that laws were only as good as their enforcement. The civil rights laws that had been established were not generally enforced because the states usually found a way to circumvent them or just simply ignore them. In 1960 a new civil right act was passed. This Act was passed in order to strengthen the enforcement section of the 1957 Act and make certain voting records were preserved. In addition, because of acts of violence associated with school desegregation, a criminal penalty was included regarding obstruction of federal court orders and bombing.

Many European Americans were dealt a severe blow to their self-images and self-worth beginning in 1964:

> The Civil Rights Act of 1964, was a watershed piece of legislation that "outlawed discrimination based on race, color, religion, sex or national origin." Originally conceived to protect the rights of black males, the bill was amended to protect the civil rights of everyone in the United States, and stipulated in no uncertain terms that women (of all races) were to be afforded the same protection.[5]

One would think that since this bill affected all Americans it would have little trouble passing Congress. President John F. Kennedy in 1963 sent the bill to Congress. However, he met his untimely death before the bill was finally approved. President Lyndon B. Johnson battled with a group of segregationists Congressmen known as the Dixiecrats who adamantly opposed the bill and even tried to defeat it through a filibuster. Of this situation, Bill Moyers states:

> Tragically, Kennedy was assassinated as Congress was still battling over his civil rights bill and Lyndon Johnson was thrust into the white House. I went with him and saw Johnson take up the cause. Martin Luther King marched, and Lyndon Johnson maneuvered, and on the 2nd of July in 1964 the President signed the Civil Rights Act into law. The fight wasn't over; he knew it. The President told me, "I think we've just handed the South to the Republican Party for the rest of my life—and yours." Sure enough, the backlash was so bitter, and the Republican Party, once the party of Lincoln, so exploited it, that I figure this country would have a serious woman candidate for President long before any person of African descent.[6]

For African Americans the Civil Rights Act of 1964, for the first time in America's history, said, in essence, that they were no longer three-fifths a man (human being), but full-fledged citizens. This acknowledgement after years of being openly discriminated against, and told they were inferior beings: "The act transformed American society by 'prohibiting discrimination in public facilities, in government, and in employment." The 'Jim Crow' laws in the South were abolished and it became illegal to force segregation of races in schools."[7] The bill was far-reaching in that

> For the first time, the act covered an entire culture — all Americans (with a few exceptions) — and it was equipped with the legislative teeth to follow through on its promises of equal treatment.

> The act barred unequal application of voter registration requirements, though it did not do away with literacy test. It also banned discrimination in hotels, motels, restaurants, theater, and other public accommodations, though it exempted private clubs. It "encouraged" the desegregation of public schools and charged the U.S. Attorney General with the filing of law suits to carry out it mandate.

> Title II of the act outlawed discrimination in employment based on race, color, creed, sex, or national origin, for any firm with 15 or more full-time employees.[8]

Since these laws were passed and resistance to them was great, some programs had to be created to implement them. So, the following year, another measure was passed — The Voting Rights Act of 1965. This bill authorized the appointment of federal examiners to register voters in places where African Americans had been greatly discriminated against. Also, the penalties for interring with voter rights were increased. In order to avoid any local problems the voter examiners were appointed by the Attorney General.

The struggle for fairness in American society was waged on many fronts. One area that stood out was housing. Since the 1954 *Brown* decision many European Americans had moved out to the suburbs where they re-segregated themselves. With a number of African Americans experiencing upward mobility through education and employment, their desire for better living conditions for themselves and their families led them to investigate the suburbs. Unfortunately, the suburbs were not ready to receive these new African American consumers. The problem became so much a concern that Congress again had to act. This action came in the form of the 1968 Civil Rights Bill that prohibited discrimination in the sale or rental of housing. Certain personal rights were also protected including attending school or working, allowing civil right workers to encourage voters to vote. In addition, anti-riot provisions were provided to help deal with the violence that had visited a number of the cities.

America has seemingly refused through the years to deal directly with it problem of bias against African Americans, as the fore mentioned civil rights bills and acts underscore. Yet, when someone mentions the lack of fairness or some symptom of slavery's legacy still visible, that person is often viewed as a villain rather than a messenger of truth. The intent of the message generally is to point out a problem so it can be addressed. Sometimes the message is heard and actions taken to remedy the problem. Unfortunately, America's race problem has avoided being realistically addressed. Certainly the topic has been discussed, but not the cause. In 1968 President Lyndon B. Johnson having experienced the violence by African Americans in the cities of Newark, New Jersey, and especially, Detroit, Michigan decided that something decisive must be done to address the problems that caused these outbreaks. He decided to appoint a commission to study the issue. Recently, (3-28-08) the noted journalist, Bill Moyers, on his television program, *Bill Moyers Journal*,[9] conducted an interview with former Senator from Oklahoma, Fred Harris, who was a member of that commission. Portions of that interview should shed some light concerning America's race problem.

Moyers began the interview by commenting on the state of affairs regarding today's atmosphere on race. He suggested that in order for an individual using the internet today and searching for the thoughts and opinions of presidential candidates regarding problems in the nation's cities, the individual would be greatly challenged. He noted that the candidate speeches have generally avoided the mention of problems involving the cities because any focus on those problems would also include the subject of race.

He explains that the subject of race was at the center of the Kerner Commission Report, but the title was actually worded to suggest civil disorders. These disorders were actually called riots and created much controversy in both the presidential campaign of 1968 as well as in society regarding the role of race. The Kerner Report, as the media called the study, was an indictment of America in that the report underscored America's lack of attention to the problems of race that contributed directly to the riots. The riots, according to Moyers, created the need for an examination of the racial problems in America, hence, the report.[10]

Moyers continued by recounting some of the history leading up to the Kerner report. He recalled, for example, "July 1967, Newark, New Jersey goes up in flames. Reacting to a rumor that police had beaten and allegedly killed a local man, residents protested peacefully at first. But then the scene turned violent." He recalled, "For six days, state troops and police clashed in the streets with rioters. Twenty-six were killed, including a ten year old boy." Another urban riot occurred six days later in Detroit, and it was worse than Newark.

Moyers noted the similarities of both riots and explained that both were in part set-off by police involvement in trying to manage protest in the center of

Detroit. He concluded that the Detroit riot was worse than the Newark one and that the total devastation of the city of Detroit was witnessed by the nation as it was displayed on television.

Moyers remembered that once the announcement was made of police coming under sniper fire in Detroit, then President, Lyndon Johnson ordered the army to go in and establish control of the situation. As a result, the army detained literally thousands of African Americans and imposed a curfew on the city.

Once the situation was under control, Moyers noted, an accounting of the damage was made that indicated Detroit was a destroyed city. The residents were faced with an inner-city that looked like the ruins of a bombed-out Europe in 1945. The riots, Moyers commented, were not restricted to Newark and Detroit, but to many other cities across the nation.[11]

Moyers indicated that because of the violence and destruction taking place in the cities, President Johnson felt compelled to act. Three basic questions, according to Johnson, needed to be answered: "What happened, why did it happen, what can be done to prevent it from happening again and again."

The President's answer was to appoint a commission: "LBJ appointed what became known as the Kerner Commission . . . named for its Chairman, Illinois Governor Otto Kerner. New York City's Mayor John Lindsay was Vice-Chair." Fred Harris, the senator from Oklahoma, thirty years old at the time was the youngest member of the panel.

Harris sits on the board of the Eisenhower Foundation based in Washington D.C. The Foundation was created to continue the Kerner Commission. Its work is to research and support successful programs in the inner cities. The interview that followed touched on the history of African Americans and European American relations leading up to the riots as well as statistics then and now that underscored the disparity between the two groups. A litany of facts were presented regarding inadequate or non-existing job, schooling, housing social agencies and programs to help alleviate the social problems affecting the inner cities in particular, and the nation's poor in general.

At this juncture in the interview with Harris, Moyers brings in a number of individuals associated with the Eisenhower Foundation for their assessment of the racial atmosphere in America. The interview continues with Moyers saying that the Eisenhower Foundation publishes a report of its finding every few years. The report is to discern how the society is addressing the issues of concerns raised by the Kerner Commission back in 1968. Moyers first speaks to Alan Curtis, the President of the Eisenhower Foundation. Curtis says he believes the problems America faces can be solved; so, we should not give up hope.

Moyers continues to speak with a number of people involved with the work of the Kerner Commission, including Komozi Woodard, Junius Williams,

Ronald Anglin and several other participants. Their collective sentiments revolve around their belief that America has never fully confronted the issues of race and prejudice. They believe that the chances for positive change is present, but will not and cannot be achieved without serious, deliberate action by all Americans, but especially European Americans.

Moyers identifies The Eisenhower Foundation as the agency that backs the on-going work of the Kerner Commission and notes that their report concludes noting that America has seen much improvement, especially with respect to the African American middle class. However, it also points out that America has yet to the goals set out in the Kerner Report, the goals to address the problems affecting Africans Americans in the nation's cities: poverty, crime, injustice etc. . . .

In additions to America is failure to address the problems set out by the report, Moyers recounted statistics that placed many African Americans at the very bottom of the economic scale. Other citizens who are not white constitute a small fraction the wealth of the white families. Also underscored in his comments is the disproportionate number of African American males incarcerated as compared to other American men.

Another person taking part in the Moyers discussion was Alan Curtis who commented on American's lack of concern for the problems for its minority population. He mentioned the lack of attention to problems facing these populations relative to drug use, the injustices in the criminal justice system, and institutional racism in general. Curtis believes that America needs not only to be constantly reminded that these problems exist but also that they should be confronted and addressed.[12]

The one concern throughout the above discussion is the fact that all of the participant believed that our nation is divided and unequal. Why do the problems first identified by the Kerner Commission still persist? Of all the possible answers to this question, the one that seems to trump the others is America does not recognize the existence of these problems. If they are not recognized, they cannot be addressed.

NOTES

1. Johnson, p. 761.
2. Johnson, p. 155.
3. Johnson, p. 155.
4. Johnson, p. 141.
5. http://www.u-shistory.com/pages/h3947.htm.
6. http://www.pbs.org/moyers/jounral/06062008/transcript.html.
7. u-shistory.

8. U-shistory.

9. *Bill Moyers Journal, PBS*, Interview with Fred Harris 3-28-2008, Public Affairs Television, New York, NY 10001 http://.pbs.org/moyers/journal/03282008/transcript3 .html p. 1.

10. Moyers, p. 3.

11. Moyers, p. 5.

12. Moyers, p. 6.

Chapter Seven

Divided Nation

Since slavery, America has been a divided nation. The division came about because of the value or lack of value placed on human beings. For those valued in society, privileges were granted by virtue of their group identity. For others, namely slaves and poor working people, little or negative value was assessed them. The negative value of the African American in the majority society continued from slavery in many ways to present day. The majority society saw little in the African American community of value except what could be exploited for profit—talent, skill, and creativity. Once those elements were exhausted, there was no need for any attention given to them. As with all human beings, the dreams, want, and needs of the African Americas were still part of their daily experiences. How were these concerns to be addressed? The answers came more often than not in the African American churches.

Because slavery and subsequent negative experiences in America attempted to rob the African American of any element of self worth or positive value, without the church no outlet for releasing the pressure and pain collected through daily life was available. The atmosphere in the church was one that encouraged freedom of expression mentally, physically, and vocally. The various positions, services, and responsibilities of the church offered the African Americans the opportunity to gain a measure of self-worth and self-value not available in general society. The church in the African American community became the hub of the activity that was vital to the life of the people in not only a religious sense, but also in social, political, economic, and educational as well.

Today many Americans do not fully understand or appreciate the impact the African American church has had and continues to have in our society.

Much change has taken place over the years in improving ethnic relations, but the impact of being a divided society still weighs heavy today. As indicated in the variety of perspectives of America by people from other countries, the knowledge and experience a person encounters helps to form their perspective. In America, because the majority society has always seen themselves as normal, and their thoughts and behavior as correct, little effort is made to try and see and understand the perspectives of other Americans, African Americans in particular. For example, how some African Americans perceive a police officer is based in large part on the experiences they have witnessed and or encountered. When ninety percent of these encounters with the police have been negative, the perception will, of course, be negative.

When the majority society is constantly presented pictures of African Americans is a negative context, those negative pictures will definitely contribute to the over-all perception of the African American by the majority. These negative perceptions affect the lives of African Americans constantly, and especially in the work place. Jobs represent one social element that indicates how far we as a society have progress. Erin Texeira, writing for the Associated Press in 2005, reported on a case involving Sodexho "Food service company Sodexho Inc. agreed Wednesday to pay $80 million to settle a lawsuit brought by thousands of black employees who charged that they were routinely barred from promotions and segregated within the company."[1] Texeira added that "The agreement, one of the biggest race-related job bias settlements in recent years, also included detailed provisions for increasing diversity at the Maryland-based company, including promotion incentives, monitoring and training."[2]

Without having to go through a litany of experiences in America that tend to keep the African American and European American communities separated, suffice it to say that many of the ideas and values regarding superiority and inferiority posited by the slavery system on the European American psyche can be readily manifested today. Those manifestations help to keep the two sides apart.

Confusion and misunderstanding is bound to exist when two sides know little about how they perceive each other, especially when one community sees everything pertaining to race as okay, while the other stills struggles for a positive self image. The one thing that can help America gain a sense of perspective is historical truth. Lonnie Kent York in his *History of Millennialism*, aptly characterized what can and does happen to a people stuck in a mid-set without the benefits of historical truth:

> Time and history have a way of either obscuring or encumbering the facts which have affected current political, moral, social or religious opinions and practices.

Often one generation will experience the upheaval of radical changes, then the next generation accepts, without reserve, those changes which have occurred through violent storms of protest. The voices of protest soon dim to faint cries against the wind, while the masses accept the change as the evidence of progress. Another generation grows to maturity imbibing the new as if it were old, being unaware of the nature or scope of what they have so easily accepted as embedded truth. To them, such opinions and practices have existed from the beginning. If they are challenged, their champions will arise to defend their practice. Such a defense will assume that the basis for their belief has always existed, therefore all should accept it without challenge. True historical facts fade into obscurity under such a defense. The error inherent in these new doctrines is thus embedded deeper into the consciousness of those who are unaware of the historical nature of their belief. Truth, then, remains only in the hearts of faithful seekers.[3]

Fortunately for America, she is a nation of seekers for wisdom and truth, although she may hesitate before heeding or following either.

NOTES

1. "Us:Sodex Settles Large Racial Bias Case," by Erin Texeira, *Associated Press,* 4-27-05. http://corpwatch.org/article.php?id=12160.
2. Texeira.
3. "History of Millennialism," Lonnie Kent York, http://www.newtestamentchurch .org/york/liberaryfiles. p. 1.

Chapter Eight

Challenges

In addressing avenues of approach to solutions to the problems of race in America, three areas of concern must be considered: perception, language, and behavior. Perception is important because it focuses on not only how we think of and view ourselves, but also how we think of and view others. The perception of the European American in American has been one of seeing themselves with the qualities of superiority, normalcy, and privilege. The perception of the European Americans towards others as seen through their laws, show a marked devaluation of human worth for African Americans in particular, and for people of color in general.

Language plays an important role in America's race problem because it is the bridge that links the perception to the word. The old saying that "sticks and stones might break my bones, but words can never hurt me," is a myth. Words have denotations and connotations, and depending on how they are used, can have a plethora of effects on the individual. Words can lift up one's emotions or bring down one's sense of value. Being careful in our choice of words can help to address the race problem.

The way we act or behave is tied to both our perceptions and language. We do not come into this work knowing how to act or behave. All human beings must learn how to adjust to their environment; therefore, someone must serve as teacher. Usually, our first teachers are our parents, but our surroundings and the people we come in contact with also serve to help us interpret how we should behave. Only when we have reached a level of understanding can we begin to evaluate our behavior based on the standards and values we have acquired from our society.

When we as a society understand our perceptions, language, and behavior relative to race, we can then proceed to the challenge. The challenge for

America is to face and accept the truth concerning race. Are we willing to continue teaching our children lies about humans being white and black? Are we willing to continue teaching them that they can be selective in choosing to believe what science has contributed to our knowledge and understanding of our world? Are we willing to try and make America a democratic society where all its citizens can enjoy the promises of life, liberty, and the pursuit of happiness?

Whether we as a society realize it or not, the rest of the world is watching us. They are looking at how we perceive one another, how we communicate with one another, and how we behave towards one another. Some are learning from us; some are evaluating us; some are judging us. We need to be mindful of our self, and the affect we have on the world through our actions at home.

Chapter Nine

Perception

If America is to address the cause of the race problem, it must challenge the perception that gives value to one group and little or none to the other. In essence, America must start seeing everyone as part of the same family, human family. Humans are not born knowing their ethnic or cultural identity. That identity comes from interaction in society. The perceptions of society are generally not challenged until something happens to call attention to something unfamiliar to us. "'Learned' perceptions, especially those derived from indirect experiences (e.g., parental, peer and academic education), may be based upon incorrect information or faulty interpretations. Since they may or may not be 'true,' perceptions are in reality—beliefs!"[1] Whether what we as humans perceive as true or not, from birth, all perceptions are given and accepted as being part of a child's identity. In his article, "Formation of In-Groups," Gordon W. Allport states:

> As early as the age of five, a child is capable of understanding that he is a member of various groups. He is capable, for example, of a sense of ethnic identification. Until he is nine or ten he will not be able to understand just what his membership signifies—how, for example, Jews differ from gentiles, or Quakers from Methodists, but he does not wait for this understanding before he develops fierce in-group loyalties.[2]

Allport is speaking about the European American child developing an identity and loyalty to his group's identity. He continues by pointing out that "Some psychologist say that the child [European American] is 'rewarded' by virtue of his membership, and that this creates the loyalty."[3] Later he adds, "A colored child is seldom or never rewarded for being a Negro—usually just the opposite, and yet he normally grows up with a loyalty to his racial group."[4] Since America was divided into two groups, Allport's comments underscore a reason for some presumed differences between African Americans and Europeans. We discover how prejudice can come into the picture. Much has to do with how one group views the other, perception and projection.

In speaking about how prejudice works in the mind, Peter Loewenberg, in his article, "The Psychology of Racism," gives an example of projection from the European American perspective:

> When forbidden desires emerge in a white man, he can facilitate their repression by projecting them onto blacks or members of other racial minorities. In the unconscious of the bigot the black represents his own repressed instincts which he fears and hates and which are forbidden by his conscience as it struggles to conform to the values professed by society. This is why the black man becomes the personification of sexuality, lewdness, laziness, dirtiness, and unbridled hostility. He is the symbol of voluptuousness and the immediate gratification of pleasure. In the deepest recesses of the minds of white Americans, Negroes are associated with lowly and debased objects or with sexuality and violence. In our society children are taught at an early age that their excrement is disgusting, smelly, and dirty, and that sexual and hostile feelings are bad and dangerous. These feelings are easily associated with low status or tabooed groups such as Negroes. Blacks are pictured in the unconscious imagery of white majority as dark and odorous, aggressive, libidinal, and threatening.[5]

What affects might these negative pictures have on African Americans and other ethnic minorities? Many of the psychological problems such as low self-esteem, self-deprecation, depression, anger, and anxiety, are known to be commonly associated with people who feel they are constantly being treated unfairly. But, what about physical effects, do they manifest themselves as well?

Lauren Dzubow, in an article, "The Sense of Being Slighted," (O The Oprah Magazine, Nov. '07) writes about the harmful physical effects of being treated unfairly. She stated that "Scientist have . . . shown that anger, depression, and anxiety predict cardiovascular problems."[6] She goes on to add that these traits trigger our reactions of fight or flight and release hormones into our bloodstream. If these hormones are activated occasionally, they are harmless, she adds, "But when kept at chronically high levels by stress, they can increase blood pressure, cholesterol, heart rate, plaque buildup, and blood clotting; adversely affect metabolism; and suppress immunity."[7] More importantly, she writes about work done by others concerning people who suffer from bias: "Researchers are now focusing on feelings of being unfairly treated, which may have a similarly detrimental effect on the heart. It doesn't seem to matter what kind of injustice one faces, or even whether it's real or imagined. What matters is our perceiving it, and how frequently."[8]

So, what this information suggests, according to the article, is that the way people are forced to perceive themselves can and do have a direct effect on their bodies:

"Discrimination can be a particularly grave threat: researchers theorize that racism might partly explain African Americans' high hypertension rate. Studies on other minority groups have also confirmed bias to be physically injurious. Jules Harrell, PhD, professor of psychology at Howard University, says that recalling or even imagining prejudice can have adverse effects on the heart. What's more, experiencing unfairness in the past can lead one to notice and expect it in the future. Brenda Major, PhD, professor of psychology at the University of California, Santa Barbara, has found that being on guard is maladaptive in benign circumstances; it raises blood pressure and engenders distrust."[9]

Later in the article, Dzubow writes where the actions of people who react directly to their being treated unfairly seem "to be linked to better health." When people who are ignorant, misinformed, or stupid make statements regarding the effects of slavery and American democracy on the African Americans like "Get over it! Slavery ended years ago," they have no ideas of the legacy created by slavery.

Although a plethora of evidence has been accumulated to support the negative effects of slavery on the African Americans, one example should suffice to demonstrate such effects. Melba Pattillo Beals, one of the young African Americans who helped to desegregate Little Rock's Central High School, writes in her memoir (*Warriors Don't Cry)* about her mental state as a child:

BLACK FOLKS ARNT BORN EXPECTING SEGREGATION, PREPARED from day one to follow its confining rules. Nobody presents you with a handbook when you're teething and says, "Here's how you must behave as a second-class citizen." Instead, the humiliating expectations and traditions of segregation creep over you, slowly stealing a teaspoonful of your self-esteem each."

By the time I was three years old, I was already so afraid of white people that when my red-haired, white-skinned cousin, Brenda, came to babysit, I hid beneath Mother's bed.[10]

As demonstrated in the excerpt above, perceptions act like and indeed are the same as beliefs. Scientific advances in our understanding of who and what we are, now help us to see what effects many of our ideas and opinions—perceptions, have on us. Because the perceptions can be viewed as beliefs Lipton states that:

> Our new scientific knowledge is returning to an ancient awareness of the power of belief. Beliefs are indeed powerful . . . whether they are true or false. While we have always heard of the "power of positive thinking," the problem is negative thinking is just as powerful, though in the "opposite direction. Problems encountered in health and in the unfolding of our lives are generally connected to the "misperceptions" acquired in our learning experiences. We can reshape our lives in retraining our consciousness.[11]

In order for America to challenge the problems of ethnic bigotry (racism), the perceptions of African Americans of themselves and those perceptions of the European Americans of African Americans must change. Accordingly, the self-perceptions of European Americans must change as well. When people view themselves or others through the prism of stereotypes, both the viewer and those being viewed are robbed of their uniqueness. All human beings must be viewed as having common positive values. Without these changes in perceptions, the problems of ethnic and cultural bias, bigotry, and prejudice in America will continue.

NOTES

1. Bruce Lipton, Human Genome Project.

2. "Formation of In-Groups," Gordon W. Allport, in *The Nature of Prejudice,* Addison-Wesley Publishing Company, 1954.

3. Allport, p. 86.

4. Allport, p. 86.

5. "The Psychology of Racism," Peter Loewenberg, in *The Great Fear: Race in the Mind of America*, edited by G.B. Nash, Holt, Rinehart & Winston, Inc. 1970, p. 115.

6. Lauren Dzubow, in an article, "The Sense of Being Slighted," (O The Oprah Magazine, Nov. '07), p. 236.

7. Dzubow, p. 236.

8. Dzubow, p. 236.

9. Dzubow, p. 236.

10. Melba Pattillo Beals, *Warriors Don't Cry*, Washington Square Press, 1995, p. 6.

11. Lipton, p. 5.

Chapter Ten

Language

The use of the terms *race* and its derivatives *racial, racist,* and the terms *white,* and *black* destroy in America the possibility of achieving equality and fairness since both terms carry with them the baggage of separateness, superiority, and inferiority. The use of these terms creates biases. Biases are based on differences that are obvious. When those differences are given values then the group with the positive values see themselves as superior to the other groups. The problem lies with the basis for the differences when no factual evidence or proof can substantiate them. In America, color is used as a difference between so-called races. However, the definition of race has nothing to do with color, only geography. Many Americans of black skin are not of immediate African descent. Are they considered part of the black race? One of the world's top golfers is Vijay Singh who happens to be of a very dark complexion, actually, a black skin. He, however, is not considered "black" because of his cultural and geographical identity. He is always referred to as a Fijian. He is a native of the Fiji Islands.

Since the definition of race does not use color as evidence of its existence, what is the logic of using color at all. What of the people with so-called "white skin" who are of African descent? Many of them have "passed" for European Americans for many years because of the privileges and benefits available to them as European Americans. Are they considered to be of the "white" race? The question begs for the use of logic or common sense.

The challenge for America in addressing the problem of race must focus some serious attention on language. The use of the terms that signal division, separateness, inferiority, and superiority have been used continuously in America since the Africans were brought to or came to these shores. The continued use of those terms simply insured the maintenance and promotion of the status quo. Since the use of these special terms became a part of America's everyday language, both the privileged and discriminated groups helped to keep the myths alive.

Paula Rothenberg in her work, *White Privilege*, talks about our problems with language:

> Increasingly, people use terms like "racism" and "sexism" to describe disparate treatment and the perpetuation of power. Yet this vocabulary of "isms" as a descriptive shorthand for undesirable, disadvantaging treatment creates several problems.
>
> First, calling someone a racist individualizes the behavior and veils the fact that racism can occur only where it is culturally, socially, and legally supported. It lays the blame on the individual rather than the systemic forces that have shaped that individual and his or her society. White people know they do not want to be labeled racist; they become concerned with how to avoid that label, rather than worrying about systemic racism and how to change it.[1]

Much progress has been made by society in general as far as providing opportunities to a large segment of ethnic minorities, especial European American women. However, society has not moved one iota in trying to close the language gap that continues to separate the ethnic Americans in general from the European Americans. For example, the language of the laws always reinforce the idea of *race* as being legitimate when they make reference to "race, color, etc. . . . ." The interpretation of these laws simply underscores the idea of there being numerous races. Addressing this problem is different for each group of African Americans and European Americans.

For the African American the challenge of finding a positive self-identity came at the beginning of American slavery. When the Africans were brought to America, the first order of business for the enslavers was to change the identity of the slaves from a positive one to a negative. The changes in identity for the African Americans follow a cyclical pattern. First, the African's identity is changes to Negro. Negro is a Latin term, which simply means black. Second, the African's identity changed to slave, i.e. African slave, Negro or black slave. Third, the African's identity is changed to slave (during this transition America began to see all Africans "Negroes" as slaves and all slaves as Negroes). Fourth, The Africans "Negroes" were identified again with Africa. However, the image of Africa had undergone a change from a beautiful, rich, and bountiful, continent, to a dark, foreboding, mysterious, habitat of cannibalizing savages. Africa began to be perceived as a place from which no self-respecting human being would want to be associated. Therefore, this place, Africa, was the home of the Negroes and their descendants. Fifth, the African Americans who were referred to as Negroes, colored, and a host of other uncomplimentary names began to reject these terms in favor of the term black. For African Americans gaining a positive identity from a socially imposed negative one are not only a tremendous challenge, but a painstaking effort as well. Finally, the learning process brought the African Americans past the black identity to that of African American.[2]

Many African Americans still hold on to the term *black* because during the cultural revolution of the 60's and 70's African Americans changed the term for themselves, from a negative value to a positive value. This move was a necessary step in the progression towards a positive self-identity. The problem with the term *black* today is that it does nothing to change the perception of the African American as separate, divided, and inferior to European Americans. No other ethnic American person of color is referred to as a color with the exception of the white and blacks. If the concern were only with the colors, no problem would exist. But, since these colors represent aspects of our historical experiences that underscore powerful mythical differences, they should be avoided.

One concern regarding language that is often avoided or not taken seriously enough is the etymology of certain words. One word of particular concern is *nigger*. April Rose Schneider in an article on the topic of the term makes the following statement:

> The origin of the word "nigger" is obscure. However, historical sources points to the Latin word "niger," which means black in English. Throughout history, "niger" experienced numerous modifications. The final version, in one sense, represents the pinnacle of historical and cultural bigotry. In hushed meetings, both public and private, and on internet web pages of 21rst century cyberspace, this word-weapon continues to perpetuate the violence of racism.[3]

Any American English dictionary will generally include the word, but each varies with respect to how the word is used. *American Heritage Dictionary* for example, lists the following: "*nigger* n. offensive Slang. A black or member of any dark-skinned people [alliteration of dial. Neger, black person<Fr. Nigre< Sp. Negro] See Negro."

When looking under the term Negro we find the following: Negro 1. A member of the Negroid ethnic division of the human species, esp. one of various peoples of central and southern Africa. A person of Negro descent [Sp. And Pot. < Negro, black < Lat. Niger.][4]

What information does these two citations provide with respect to the African American? We learned quite some time earlier that scientists discontinued the use of the terms Negroid, Caucasoid, and Mongoloid, yet the citation for Negro uses the term *Negroid* to identify a specific people. To the uninformed reader, the term labels all people of dark complexion. Society adds the negative context.

Another term commonly used to identify people of the so-called white race is *Caucasian. The American Heritage Dictionary* list the following information relative to this term: "Caucasian *adj.* 1.Of or being a purported human racial classification traditionally distinguished by light to brown skin color and including people indigenous to Europe, N Africa, W Asia, and India. Not in scientific use. 2. Of the Caucasus,—*n.* 1. A member of the Caucasian racial classification. 2. A native or inhabitant of the Caucasus."[5]

Based on this dictionary information, the people who can be identified as Caucasian or white do not have to be of a white complexion. Also, since the scientific community no longer accepts these racial classifications, they serve no useful purpose except to separate and divide people. No one should expect an overnight change in our use of bias language, and no one should expect to see biases and bigotry disappear because we begin to avoid and discontinue use of certain inappropriate terms. The process of change will be a gradual one.

The language must change if further progress is to be made. However, effecting a change of language represents a major challenge. When people are not sufficiently informed about the need or desire to change language than work must be done to bring them into an understanding of why the change is needed. For example, a number of states have offered apologies for their historical involvement in the system of slavery. These states include Alabama, Maryland, North Carolina and Virginia. The apology indicates an understanding of the legacy and consequences of that system on the American society, not that the apology in and of itself will physically change anything—but it will show that at least some thought has gone into society's understanding of the experience.

In New Jersey, a congressman who wants the state to make an apology for slavery using only three words, "we are sorry" has created a controversy. Assemblyman William Payne, the sponsor of the proposal, indicated, "New Jersey had one of the largest slave populations in the Northern colonies and was the last state in the Northeast to formally abolish slavery, not doing so until 1846."[6]

Opposition to this proposal comes from in particular, Assemblyman Richard Merkt who asked the questions "Who living today is guilty of slave holding and thus capable of apologizing for the offense?" He adds, "And who living today is a former slave and thus capable of accepting the apology? So how is a real apology even remotely possible, much less meaning?"[7]

What we recognize as missing from the response and questions of Assemblyman Merkt is an understanding of the effects slavery had and continues to have on American society. The picture of slavery held by Mr. Merkt seems to suggest that it was a fad that has passed leaving no serious or lasting negative impact on society. In essence, since slaves and slaver owners no longer exist in America, why bring up the past. Language was the vehicle that created the views that both Assemblymen Payne and Merkt have of slavery and society; and language was used to explain and clarify the issue. New Jersey accepted the proposal and offered its apology for slavery.

NOTES

1. Paula S. Rothenberg, *White Privilege: essential readings on the other side of racism*, 2nd edition, Worth Publishers, 2005, p. 97.

2. For a detailed discussion on this subject see: *The Making of the Negro in Early American Literature*, Paul R. Lehman, Fountainhead Press, 2006.

3. "Nigger," April Rose Schneider, http://racism-politics.suite101.com/article.cfm/nigger).

4. *The American Heritage Dictionary*, Second College Edition, Houghton Mifflin Company, 1982, p. 836.

5. *The American Heritage Dictionary*, p. 249.

6. "Apology may be first for North," *The Associate Press, The Oklahoman*, 1-3-08, p. 4A.

7. Apology, 4A.

Chapter Eleven

Behavior

Following perception, language is the third element, behavior. America has shown through its behavior how it values its African American citizens. That behavior was transmitted through the law society created and enforced. A good example of America's behavior can be seen through the laws that were established in the various states prior to the Civil War. In a trail-blazing work of research and dedication, Lydia Maria Child published *An Appeal in Favor of That Class of Americans Called Africans.*[1] This work came at great cost to Child in that she went against the grain of popular thought by choosing to refer to the African/ African Americans as Africans rather than Negro, Colored, black. She knew the power of a positive self-identity. Before this publication, Child had an application submitted to a prestigious Boston Literary organization, once the work came out; Child's application was withdrawn by the organization.

In any event, this publication contained laws, states, and dates were made public regarding the treatment of slaves. The intent was to show the lack of human compassion inherent in the system of slavery. For this purpose, she examines fourteen points of law as follows:

1. Slavery is hereditary and perpetual, to the last moment of the slave's earthly existence, and to all his descendants, to the latest posterity.
2. The labor of the slave is compulsory and uncompensated; while the kind of labor, the amount of toil, and the time allowed for rest, are dictated solely by the master. No bargain is made, no wages given. A pure despotism governs the human brute; and even his covering and provender, both as to quantity and quality, depend entirely on the master's discretion.

3. The slave being considered a personal chattel, may be sold, or pledged, or leased, at the will of his master. He may be exchanged for marketable commodities, or taken in execution for the debts, or taxes, either of a living, or deceased master. Sold at auction, "either individually, or in lots, to suit the purchaser," he may remain with his family, or be separated from them forever.

4. Slaves can make no contracts, and have no legal right to any property, real or personal. Their own honest earnings, and the legacies of friends belong, in point of law, to their masters.

5. Neither a slave, or free colored person can be a witness against any white or free man, in a court of justice, however atrocious may have been the crimes they have seen him commit: but they may give testimony against a fellow-slave, or free colored man, even in cases affecting life.

6. The slave may be punished at his master's discretion–without trial—without any means of legal redress,—whether his offence be real, or imaginary; and the master can transfer the same despotic power to any person, or persons, he may choose to appoint.

7. The slave is not allowed to resist any free man under any circumstances: his only safety consists in the fact that his owner may bring suit, and recover, the price of his body, in case his life is taken, or his limbs rendered unfit for labor.

8. Slaves cannot redeem themselves, or obtain a change of masters, though cruel treatment may have rendered such a change necessary for their personal safety.

9. The slave is entirely unprotected in his domestic relations.

10. The laws greatly obstruct the manumission of slaves, even where the master is willing to enfranchise them.

11. The operation of the laws tends to deprive slaves of religious instruction and consolation.

12. The whole power of the laws is exerted to keep slaves in a state of the lowest ignorance.

13. There is in this country a monstrous inequality of law and right. What is a trifling fault in the white man, is considered highly criminal in the slave; the same offences which cost a white man a few dollars only, are punished in the negro with death.

14. The laws operate most oppressively upon free people of color.[2]

In her explanations, Child goes into detail in discussing how the behavior of the slaves and their enslavers are affected. For example, in Proposition #7—The slave is never allowed to resist a white man, she states:

It is enacted in Georgia, "If any slave shall presume to strike *any* white man, such slave, upon trial and conviction before the justice, shall for the *first* offence, suffer punishment as the said justice thinks fit, not extending to life or limb; and for the second offence, *death*." It is the same in South Carolina, excepting that death is there the punishment of the *third* offence. However wanton and dangerous the attack upon the slave may be, he must submit; there is only one proviso—he may be excused for striking in defence of his *master, overseer, etc.*, and *their* property. In Maryland, a colored man, even if he be *free*, may have his ears cropped for striking a white man. In Kentucky, it is enacted that "if any Negro, mulatto, or Indian, bond or *free*, shall at any time lift his or her hand, in opposition to *any* person not colored, they shall, the offence being proved before a justice of the peace, receive thirty lashes on his or her bare back, well laid on." There is a ridiculous gravity in the following section of a law in Louisiana: "Free people of color ought never to insult to strike white people, nor presume to conceive themselves equal to the whites; but on the contrary, they ought to yield to them *on every occasion*, and never speak or answer to them but with respect, under the penalty of imprisonment, according to the nature of the offence."

Such laws are a positive *inducement* to violent and vicious white men to oppress and injure people of color. In this point of view, a Negro becomes the slave of every white man in the community. The brutal drunkard, or the ferocious madman, can beat, rob, and mangle him with perfect impunity. Dr. Torrey, in his "Portraiture of Domestic Slavery," relates an affecting anecdote, which happened near Washington. A free Negro walking along the road, was set upon by two intoxicated ruffians on horseback, who, without any provocation, began to torture him for *amusement*. One of them tied him to the tail of his horse, and thus dragged him along, while the other fellow, applying the lash. The poor fellow died by the roadside, in consequence of this treatment.[3])

The obvious points of these examples are to underscore how the perceptions, and language (law), affect the behavior of the society. The fact that these laws and behavior predates modern Civil Rights laws one might suspect that great change has taken place in society since American society in better informed and more enlightened than before the Civil War. The fact is that some of society has experienced a positive change in its behavior, but much of the sentiment of being white and privileged continues to rear it ugly head in many areas of American life today. One has only to pick up a newspaper, turn on a radio or television to learn of some behavior that fits the pattern of the pre Civil War years.

Behavior of both African Americans and European Americans in today's society represents a major concern for each segment of society. Common sense dictates that when a person is knowledgeable about something the better able he or she is in making decisions about that thing. In essence, knowledge is power. When people experience upward mobility, their lives change in accordance with what they determine best suits their needs. The decisions are generally based on socioeconomic status rather than color or ethnicity. In the 1960s and 1970s when the nation was experiencing "white flight" to the suburbs, many African Americans also took the opportunity to move to the suburbs. Unfortunately, their European American neighbors believed that they, the European Americans, were the reason for the African Americans moving. The truth was that the African Americans moved to the suburbs for socioeconomic reasons—a better life for themselves and their families. Although the behavior of each group was the same, moving to the suburbs, their reasons for doing so were very different.

The welcome many African Americans received when moving to some suburbs was anything but friendly. Part of the feeling of being privileged is to be set apart from people thought to be inferior. When that sense of privilege is threatened, the reactions of the affected party can and often is violent and abusive. African Americans were the recipients of that violence and abuse. Even when African Americans lived in separate communities they were not safe from the bigoted control of the European Americans. One example stands out very clearly, that of the Tulsa Race Riot of 1921.

The Greenwood community, across the railroad tracks from the European American section of Tulsa, Oklahoma, was viewed as a tribute to the success of American democracy in that this very prosperous community was the home of several thousand African Americans. What happened to the Greenwood community is a matter of history, which has been recorded in numerous book and articles. One book in particular, *The Burning,* tells of Tim Madigan, the author's first knowledge of the event:

> I was oblivious to Tulsa's historic nightmare until that day in the winter of 2000 when Julie Heaberlin, my editor at the *Fort Worth Star-Telegram*, stopped by my desk in the Features Department. It was then that Julie handed me a copy of a short wire-service story about the Tulsa Race Riot Commission, which had been created a few years before to study a particularly deadly racial outbreak in 1921. As many as three hundred people had been killed in the catastrophe, the wire story said, most of the victims black. A uniquely prosperous community of African Americans, called Greenwood—thirty-five square block and literally thousands of home, businesses, churches, and schools—had been obliterated by a white mob in Tulsa that numbered in the thousands.[4]

The book tells of the police, fire, and sheriff's department's help in the destruction of the Greenwood community. In addition, help for the destruction of this community also came from the Oklahoma National Guard, and the Ku Klux Klan. Many African Americans ran for their lives. The police and other civic-minded citizen rounded up those who could not escape:

> As the white advanced across the black quarter, a Tulsa motorcycle cop named Leo Irish strung a long rope through the belt loops of six black men, hooked one end onto his motorcycle, then hopped on his machine and double-timed the prisoners on a mile-long trot from Greenwood to Convention Hall. It was among the more infamous means of transporting black prisoners on that morning when thousands of Negroes—men, women and children of all ages and from every strata of Greenwood life—were captured and marched by whites to the Convention Hall; then, when the hall was full, on to the local baseball stadium called McNulty Park. Whites stepped from their houses and businesses and cheered at the sight of all those Negroes under guard with their hands in the air.[5]

Numerous writers today use the Tulsa Race Riot as an example of extreme bias and control by European Americans towards African Americans. One writer in particular, Rilla Askew, wrote a historical fiction novel, *Fire in Beulah*,[6] using the Tulsa riot as the historical base of her story. She underscores in the plot that two myths dominate American society from the very beginning—one of European superiority, and the belief in races. In an article by Kenneth Hada, "The power to undo sin: race, history and literary blackness in Rilla Askew's *Fire in Beulah*," he states that

> Askew's philosophical assumptions are Christian, and this somewhat sets her apart from many other contemporary writers of literary fiction. She overtly uses the terms "repentance" and "sin," yet her story is neither sentimental nor evangelistic. She weaves these Christian terms into a realistic narrative that challenges any presupposed notion of their efficacy. At the end of the novel, it is still unclear to what extent repentance occurs within the main character, Althea. Askew's imaging of the evil inherent within the racial conflict, however, clearly establishes the need for individual and collective repentance. While her prose is lyrical, similar to that of Cormac McCarthy, her plots and dialogue are harsh, though not as consistently graphic as McCarthy's. What she primarily has in common with McCarthy and others, however, is the virtual undoing of the supposed ethics of a dominant white race that encounters pre-existing cultures within the American frontier.[7]

The behavior of the good people of Tulsa (we can view Tulsa as representative of the American society) indeed, the leaders of the state from the governor down to the men in the streets during this sad experience shows the hypocrisy of American democracy as reflected in the African American and the European characters in the novel.

What still remains a puzzle in Askew's work, however, is where were all the so-called democratic-minded, Christian, God-fearing, European American citizens of Tulsa during this catastrophe? Where were they after the riot? Where are they today? Once again, we see that behavior speaks volumes. Unfortunately, because both myths of race and superiority have been around for so long until many Americans believe they are true. As a matter of fact, the most obvious difficult challenge for America to recognize is that all people are of one race, the human race.

Revisiting many of the recorded instances of inhumane treatment of African Americans through legal as well as illegal means would not be difficult to do. America has consistently shown through behavior how little it values African Americans. Following the Civil War, laws were created to maintain the status of the African Americans that existed prior to their freedom. Laws continued to give privilege to the European Americans; however, the penalties by law were not as severe as before the Civil Rights era. Nevertheless, the laws could not prevent the biases, prejudices, bigotry, discrimination, violence and death visited on the African Americans by the privileged majority society.

A more recent example of bias behavior towards African Americans and other minorities can be seen in an article entitled "Whites more likely to get narcotics in emergency rooms, study find," by the *Associated Press*, (*The Oklahoman,* 1-2-08, p.13A). The article underscores the finding of a study that indicated whites received privileged treatment in many emergency rooms cases:

> *CHICAGO*—Emergency room doctors are prescribing strong narcotics more often to patients who complain of pain, but minorities are less likely to get them than whites, a new study finds.
>
> Even for the severe pain of kidney stones, minorities were prescribed narcotics such as oxycodone and morphine less frequently than whites.[8]

The article continues by stating that more than 150,000 emergency room cases over a period of 13 years found differences in the way patients were treated in hospitals, both urban and rural and for a variety of pain. The article more specifically stated that:

> "The gaps between whites and nonwhites have not appeared to close at all," said study co-author Dr. Mark Pletcher of the University of California, San Francisco.
>
> The study appears in today's *Journal of the American Medical Association*. Prescribing narcotics for pain in emergency rooms rose during the study from 23 percent of those complaining of pain in 1993 to 37 percent in 2005.

The increase coincided with changing attitudes among doctors who now regard pain management as a key to healing. Doctors in accredited hospitals must ask patients about pain, just as they monitor vital signs such as temperature and pulse.

Even with the increase, the racial gap endured. Linda Simoni-Wastila of the University of Maryland, Baltimore, School of Pharmacy said the race gap finding may reveal some doctors' suspicions that minority patients could be lying about pain to get narcotics.

The irony, she said, is that blacks are the least likely group to abuse prescription drugs.[9]

The thousands of studies that attempted to prove that somehow African Americans were born with genes inferior to European Americans have been disproved. According to Bruce H. Lipton,

Over the last number of years, science and the press' emphasis on the "power" of genes has overshadowed the brilliant work of many biologist that reveal a radically different understanding concerning organismal expression. Emerging at the cutting edge of cell science is the recognition that the environment, and more specifically, our perception of the environment, directly controls our behavior and gene activity.[10]

Clearly, the behavior as indicated in this article reflects some of the preconceived ideas and attitudes in society regarding the value of African Americans in comparison to European Americans (whites). Behavioral biases can be subtle or blatant and society will never eliminate them completely, but being consciously aware of them helps to identify a starting point from which to begin work.

Regarding behavior, the one American institution to have the most profound influence on our divided society is the church. As in other institutions, the church in America has been divided into two segments: African American and European American. History tells us that some slave masters permitted the slaves to have a religious service on Sundays. These services were generally conducted by an European American initially. The subject and text of the messages were restricted those parts of the Bible that underscored the slaves obedience to the master. For example, Saint Paul in his letter to the Ephesians (6.5-6): "Servants, be obedient to them that are your masters according to the flesh, with fear and trembling, in singleness of your heart, as unto Christ."[11] Or as in Paul's letter to the Colossians (3.22-25):

22. Servants, obey in all things your masters According to the flesh; not with eyeservice, as Menpleasers;but in singleness of heart, fearing God:
23. And whatsoever ye do, do it heartly, as to The Lord, and not unto men;

24. Knowing that of the Lord ye shall receive The reward of the inheritance: for ye serve the Lord Christ.

25. But he that doeth wrong shall receive for The wrong which he hath done: and there is no Respect of persons.[12]

(Holy Bible, King James Version,)

What the slave masters prevented the preachers from sharing with the slaves was the message intended for the masters and how they should treat their slaves. The purpose of allowing the slaves to hear the word of God was to make them better slaves. What the masters did not realize was that in allowing the slaves a religious service, the slaves gained a small measure of hope and self-esteem.

Later, when the master felt comfortable in letting one of his slaves conduct the meeting, he did not realize that these meetings provided an opportunity for the slaves to work together and create plans of action relative to their situation. Whether these plans involved escaping, destruction of property or insurrection, they were often made right under the master's nose. The master did not fully trust the slave preacher, so a spy was embedded among the audience so any plans involving rebellion would be reported to the master. The slave preachers were aware of the possibility of spies being present, so they manipulated their language to serve a variety of purposes as the situation dictated. These activities became very important in the later development of the church for African Americans. God and the church did not serve the same purposes when compared to the purposes of the European Americans. When one group is enslaved and down-trodden the need, wants and requests from God and His church are quite different from those of the group enslaving and controlling. Hence, the primary difference between the two churches is deliverance from an earthly hell versus praise and thanksgiving for all the blessings received through slavery.

The church environment was often the place where behavior was underscored in both the African American and European American communities. For African Americans learning to live in a biased society was a necessity because at time as the consequences of ignorance was death. The African American church offered information and instruction to its members on how to navigate through the critical barriers presented by the majority society. Religious teaching was not the church's sole purpose; the entire lives of the members were equally important.

For the European American, the church represented a different experience when compared to the African American experience. Since European Americans set the standards for all America, those standards were communicated through the church. The perspective of the church members was always one of superiority over non-Europeans. When someone not of European identity exhibited behavior contrary to what European Americans viewed as normal, comments, and often actions were taken to correct the behavior. The bias of American society did not appear over night, it was cultivated in the society with the church serving as the primary vehicle regarding proper behavior.

Throughout slavery the majority churches continued to follow the biased behavior it had created, promoted, and maintained. In 1850 the Baptist Church in America split and the Southern Baptist was created. The primary reason for the break-up was slavery. Pat Gilliland, Religion Editor for the *Daily* Oklahoman (1995), writes about the Southern Baptists statement of reconciliation concerning their involvement in perpetuating slavery:

> But first, "messengers" sent by churches in the nation's largest non-Catholic denomination will observe their 150th anniversary by attempting to make amends for harm done since the group was born out of a split with northern Baptists over southern approval of slavery.
> "There's no question that the issue of slavery was part of our beginning 150 years ago," said the Rev. Anthony Jordan, pastor of Northwest Baptist Church in Oklahoma. But, he said, "that's not what we stand for."[13]

The southern Christian slaveholders believed that slavery of Africans was a God-given right, and since the culture and wealth of the South had been built on the backs of the slaves, the economy of the South depended on the labor of the slaves. Therefore, giving up slavery was not a consideration.

The influence of the church (not to single out the Baptists) on the behavior of many European Americans regarding race is incalculable. The biased influence of the European American church-goers was not restricted to local pastors and congregations. The introduction of Charles Darwin's work came into play regarding the justification for biases against African Americans. Paul R. Griffin, in his *Seeds of Racism*, writes that

> Human nature, according to Darwin, was not final or finished but was constantly evolving from lower (or animal) characteristics to higher (or more human) characteristics. Christians of the time, especially biblical literalists, should have rejected Darwinian evolution as blasphemy against God—and more than a few fundamentalist and liberal Christians did. Many others, however, just as readily and vigorously turned his hypotheses into a theological-scientific argument against black humanity.

> The latter racist Christians were aided by two highly acclaimed figures in the history of American Christianity. Indeed, the racism of the Reverend Josiah Strong and the Reverend Walter Rauschenbusch has been all but ignored. Yet, it

is from the writings of these two men that we may see more clearly how intellectuals among the clergy wove Darwin's scientific ideas into their own racist theological bias.[14]

As a democratic society America likes to think of itself as continuing to grow and progress in treating all its citizens fairly. However, when the behavior of the majority citizens continue to reflect a bias, the question of change seems not to be taken seriously.

NOTES

1. Lydia Maria Child, *An Appeal in Favor of That Class of Americans Called Africans*, Umass Press: Amherst 1996.

2. Child, p. 40.

3. Child, p. 50.

4. Tim Madigan, *The Burning, Massacre, Destruction, and the Tulsa Race Riot of 1921*, Thomas Dunne Books, 2002, p. xiii.

5. Madigan, p. 138–139.

6. Rilla Askew, *Fire in Beulah*, Penguin Books, 2002.

7. Kenneth Hada, "The power to undo sin: race, history and literary blackness in Rilla Askew's *Fire in Beulah*," *College Literature, Fall* (2007), p. 2.

8. "Whites more likely to get narcotics in emergency rooms, study find," *The Associated Press (The Oklahoman) 1-2-08*.

9. "White more likely . . .,"p. 13A.

10. Lipton, p. 4

11. Ephesians (6.5-6): *Holy Bible,(King James Version)THOMAS Nelson Inc. 1977*

12. Colossians (3.22-25): *Holy Bible,(King James Version,)*

13. "Baptist to look at Restructuring, Racism Issues," Pat Gilliland, *The Daily Oklahoma , 6-19-1995*.

14. Paul R. Griffin, *Seeds of Racism in the Soul of America*, Sourcebooks, Inc. Illinois, 2000.

Chapter Twelve

The Race Box

The relationships among perception, language, and behavior, not necessarily in that order, are so close that discerning the end of one and the beginning of the other is often difficult if not impossible to do consistently. One thing is certain, however, they all play a major role in America's problem with race, and if that problem is to be effectively addressed, those three elements must be considered in the first order of business. We said at the beginning of our discussion that the problem with race in America is race. That is, the use of the word *race*. Once we introduce that word into our language, we become controlled by it.

Many Americans are hesitant to talk about the subject of race. They are hesitant because any discussion will make them feel uneasy or vulnerable about the interpretation of the word in conversation. No one wants to be viewed as bias or prejudice when conversing with others, so the best way to not feel uneasy is to avoid the subject altogether. Sometimes, however, avoiding the subject of race is not possible. What many people come to realize is that they know very little about race. Their actions and reactions regarding race come from their social experiences. More often than not, those experiences are based on false assumptions and information. The catchword is race.

Getting caught in a discussion about race begins with the word race. Picture a room with a freshly painted floor. Nothing in the room is out of order with the exception of the wet floor. Once one enters the room, however, the wet paint adheres to the sole of the shoes. Everywhere the one goes in that room he or she will be moving with the paint on the bottom of his or her shoes. Only the imprint of the shoes can be seen on the floor because the floor and paint are the same color. Regardless of what the person does, or where he or she goes in that room, the paint remains of the shoes. In order to remove the paint from the shoes, the person must exit the room and immediately take off or clean the shoes or paint will be tracked wherever he or she goes.

The word race as used in America is like that room with wet paint on the floor. Once we enter the room, we cannot extricate ourselves from the paint and everything that is said and done in that room. In essence, the room and the paint on the floor control us. One effective way of avoiding the race box or the subject of race is to not walk into the room by using the word *race*. We have more accurate terms of identification that helps us avoid the pitfall of race — African American, European American, ethnic, ethnicity, to mention a few.

Many Americans have become comfortable with the word race to the point that it is accepted without question. Life in America for them involves acquiescing to the ramifications of the social positions race dictates. Any discussion of race involves the terms *white* and *black*. Regardless of where the discussion goes, the underpinning of preference and bias goes as well. In essence, people place themselves in a box and ignore the word around them that exists outside of the box. Certainly life inside the box can be explained and rationalized because all the conditions are given. Outside the box, however, is a totally different world. Outside the box, we know the limits of the word race, but we choose to ignore it.

America operates inside the race box, and because it does, everything is viewed as either black or white. As we discussed earlier, white is normal and privileged, black is inferior and not privileged. A brief glance at American fiction will underscore that fact. If we were to look at any of the great works written by African Americans about African Americans we would quickly discover that one of the key concerns in those works has to do with self-identity and/or self-value. Both of these concerns were created inside America's race box. The normal image of the African American as viewed through the race box is one of a stereotype with negative connotations. For example, when Ralph Ellison's *Invisible Man* opens we learn from the narrator's grandfather that the primary game for the African American in America is "Who am I?"[1] The narrator goes through the entire book looking for a positive self-image. What he discovers, however, is that society has no positive self-image for African Americans because everything is seen through the prism of race. The literature reflects society in the race box.

When an African American who does not fit the European American stereotype of him comes to public attention, then that African American is seen as being *different*. What is meant by being *different* are the elements of character exhibited by the African American that transcends the racial stereotypes and invade the level of normalcy reserved for the European Americans. For European Americans to see African Americans as normal is an extremely difficult challenge because society has done such a through job of picturing him in a negative stereotype throughout his American experience. For example, one medium that has contributed to that negative stereotype of the African American but in a subtle way is animation. Christopher P. Lehman, in his book, *The Colored Cartoons*, offers the following comments on this subject:

> American animation owes its existence to African Americans. This is not to suggest that African Americans were involved in the technological development of animated film or even that they played an active role in the creation of the first cinematic cartoon. The connection between African Americans and animation was more subtle and indirect than that but nonetheless intimate and unmistakable. Early cartoons are replete with African American characters and caricatures, and such images soon became a staple of this new cultural medium. One of the first cartoons ever made in the United States, James Stuart Blackton's *Lightning Sketches* (1907), featured the metamorphosis of a racial epithet—the word "coon"—into a pair of eyes on a blackface caricature, and Metro-Goldwyn— Mayer (MGM) produced films starring a recurrent "mammy" character for over a decade. Other popular cartoon figures, such as Felix the Cat, Mickey Mouse, and Bugs Bunny, were less derogatory, but they too traced their roots to African American culture.[2]

If we were to ask the question, why would the interpretation of the African American culture and characters be appropriate and/or acceptable for ridicule in cartoon, Lehman answer would be "Simple racism, a deeply ingrained tradition in the United States. . . ."

Inside America's race box many of the great fictional works written by European Americans that include African American characters, usually picture them as stereotypical or extraordinary. Normal for the African American character is a negative stereotype. In *Uncle Tom's Cabin*, the "good" Negro, Uncle Tom, dies at the end; but he dies a Christian. The "bad" Negro, Jim Harris, escapes to Canada and freedom. Although he constantly defied the system of slavery forced upon him, at the story's end, he joins his family in Canada, and as far as we know, lives happy ever after. Uncle Tom, unfortunately, dies, but as a Christian, and never knowing his true identity. He accepted the identity given him without question. Jim Harris, one the other hand, learned the game society was playing with the identity of the African Americans slaves. He played the game long enough for him to win. He never accepted the identity society tried to force on him.[3]

The African Americans like other ethnic Americans become more likeable and acceptable to American society the more like the European American they become. As someone once said, imitation is the sincerest form of flattery. While the African American and other ethnic Americans might see themselves as acquiring behavior consistent with American culture, others might seen them as trying to imitate the European American. The imitation is good only to a point. The imitators should always remember to pay deference to the superior European American, never think they are on the same social or economic level. If that should happen, by mistake, of course, the European American will put the imitators in their place for acting uppity. In essence, they are different from the usual stereotype associated with their ethnic identity, but they are not equal to the European Americans.

Inside America's race box the word race and it many derivatives have meaning that do not apply outside the box. The word racist, for example, only has meaning inside the race box. Outside the box, who would be characterized as racist? Certainly no human being would be viewed in that light because what other race would be available for contrasting? If our science and intellect tells us that only one race of man exist, than either all humans are racist or none are. Although the challenge for America to step outside of the race box is difficult, the experience would be liberating for everyone because presently everyone is viewed through race. Both the African Americans and European Americans would be emancipated from the intellectual slavery controlling them since the beginning of this society. The acknowledgement of the fact that all humans belong to the same family should help to relieve the guilt felt by many European Americans concerning fairness in society. A new definition of normalcy should go far in eliminating the privileges afforded the European Americans.

For the African American, stepping outside the race box would present a new self-image, one that does not carry with it a negative value. Certainly, discrimination will still exist, but not on the same level as inside the race box. The new level of discrimination and biases cannot use as support elements that are inherent, because we are all members of the same family. The thousands of studies that attempted to prove that somehow African Americans were born with genes inferior to European Americans have been disproved. Tony Fitzpatrick, in an article related to this point, writes about the work of Alan R. Templeton, Ph.D., professor of biology in Arts and Sciences; he states:

> Using the latest molecular biology techniques, Templeton has analyzed millions of genetic sequences found in three distinct types of human DNA and concluded that, in the scientific sense, there is no such thing as race.
>
> "Race is a real cultural, political and economic concept in society, but it is not a biological concept, and that unfortunately is what many people wrongfully consider to be the essence of race in human—genetic differences," Templeton said. "Evolutionary history is the key to understanding race, and new molecular biology techniques offer so much on recent evolutionary history. I want to bring some objectivity to the topic. This very objective analysis shows the outcome is

not even a close call: There's nothing even like a really distinct subdivision of humanity.[4]

The major challenge for America in addressing the race problem is to recognize and acknowledge the fact that discrimination and biases were elements woven into the fabric of American life from the beginning. All Americans were and are affected by the phenomena. Several hundred years have passed and while society has made some progress with respect to granting rights and privileges to European American men and women, as well as other ethnic Americans, the legacy of slavery, the race problem, has never been appropriately addressed. The discussion always begins with race, and that beginning spells is doom.

The founding father, Thomas Jefferson, played a trick on us when he wrote in the *Declaration of Independence* that "All men are created equal," because he knew then as we know now that "equal" is a mathematical term, not a social one. He probably also knew that no one would challenge the word at the time. Equality is impossible for humans if taken on an individual bases. What would be offered as an instrument of measurement? Equal treatment must be given to individuals, and not a state of being. For example, many parents believe they treat their children equally, but this is not the case even if all the children were of the same sex. If the children were boys and girls, then to treat them equally from a materialistic sense would require the parents to purchase the same items for both sexes in the same number at the same time. To do less, would not be equal treatment. Most people, once they understand the significance of "equal" would probably agree that all people want to be treated fairly, not equally.

The idea associated with the word equal is one that allows for the powers that be to value each individual the same or equally, not that each individual is equal to the other, but that each individual is given the same value as in "life, liberty and the pursuit of happiness." Unfortunately, all Americans have not been treated equally or fairly, and that has been at the center of America's social problems.

America is faced with a choice: to live inside the race box as it does presently, or to move outside of it and start to address some of the problems created by the separation and division it causes.

A recent PBS program, *Race: the power of an illusion,* listed ten things America should know and address if we are serious about bigotry and ethnic bias:

1. Race is a modern idea. Ancient societies, like the Greeks, did not divide people according to physical distinctions but according to religion, status, class, even language.

2. Race has no genetic basis. Not one characteristic, trait or even gene distinguishes all the members of one so-called race from all the members of another so-called race.

3. Human subspecies don't exist. Unlike many animals, modern humans simply haven't been isolated or around long enough to evolve into separate subspecies or races. We are one of the most similar of all species.

4. Skin color really is only skin deep. Most traits are inherited independently from one another. The genes influencing skin color have nothing to do with those influencing hair form, eye shape, blood type, musical talent, athletic ability or forms of intelligence.

5. Most variation is within, not between, "races." Of the small amount of total human variation, 85% exists within any local population—e.g., Italians, Koreans or Cherokees. About 94% exists within any continent. Two random Koreans may be genetically different as a Korean and an Italian.

6. Slavery predates race. For much of human history, societies have enslaved others, often as a result of conquest, even debt, but not because of physical traits or a belief in natural inferiority. Due to a unique set of historical circumstances, ours was the first system where all slaves shared similar physical characteristics [this statement is true only after all Africans and their progeny represented the slave system. Prior to that, Europeans, Indians, and Africans were enslaved.].

7. Race and freedom evolved together. The U.S. was founded on the radical new principle that "All men are created equal." But our early economy was based largely on slavery. The new idea of race helped rationalize why some people could be denied the rights and freedoms that others took for granted.

8. Race justified social inequalities as natural. As the race idea evolved white superiority became "common sense" in the U.S. It helped justify slavery, Indian conquest, the exclusion of Asian immigrants, and the taking of Mexican lands in spite of our belief in democracy and freedom. Racial practices were institutionalized within U.S. government, laws, and society.

9. Race isn't biological, but racism is real. Race is a powerful social idea that gives people different access to opportunities and resources. Our government and social institutions have created advantages that disproportionately channel wealth, power, and resources to white [European American] people. This [advantage] affects everyone, whether we are aware of it or not.

10. Colorblindness will not end racism. Pretending race doesn't exist is not the same as creating equality. To combat racism, we need to identify and remedy social policies and institutional practices that advantage some groups at the expense of others.[5]

If American is to address its race problem, it will have to go outside of the box.

NOTES

1. Ralph Ellison, *Invisible Man,* Vintage International, 1995.

2. Christopher P. Lehman, *The Colored Cartoon: Black Representation in American Animated Short Films, 1907-1954,* University of Massachusetts Press, 2007, p. 1.

3. Harriet Beecher Stowe, *Uncle Tom's Cabin,* Bantam Books, 1989.

4. "Biological differences among races do not exist, WU research shows," Tony Fitzpatrick. Alan R. Templeton, Ph.D., professor of biology, article on DNA is subject discussed in this paper. http://record.wustl.edu/archive/1998/10-15-98/articles/race.html, p. 1.

5. PBS program, *Race: the power of an illusion*, California Newsreel Web site: www.newsreel.org.

Index

African: ape and, 11; intellectual
inferiority of, 22; positive to negative
change of, 56–57; slaves, 13; worth
of, 29–30
African Americans: America treatment
of, viii–ix, 35, 56–57; bias against,
39–40; cartoon animation and, 73;
churches of, 45–46, 67, 68;
European Americans bigoted
control of, 64; housing for, 39; on
inferior genes of, 67; negative
stereotypes of, v, 56–57, 73;
negative value of, 45–46, 66, 74; as
presidential candidate, v; self-
identity of, 56; violence against, v,
63, 66; worth of, 29–30. *See also*
black; slave; slavery
Allport, Gordon W., 51–52
America: African American treatment
by, viii–ix, 35, 56–57; citizen races
of, 4–5; comments on, vi–vii; as
divided nation, 45–47; ethnic bigotry
in, xi; patriotic songs of, viii;
Pilgrims/Puritans and, 11; in race
box, 71–77; race discussion by, 71;
world presentation of, vii
The American Heritage Dictionary, 57,
58

American Indians, enslavement of, 10,
13
ancestry, English on, 3
Anglin, Ronald, 42
*An Appeal in Favor of That Class of
Americans Called Africans* (Child),
61
Article I, section 2, of Constitution, viii
The Aryan Nations, 22
Aryan race, 7
Askew, Rilla, 65–66
Associated Press, 66–67

Baptist Church, 69. *See also* Southern
Baptist Church
Barzan, Jacques, 1, 2
BBC News, America comments
solicited by, vi–vii
Beals, Melba Pattillo, 53
behavior, 49, 61–71; law transmittal of,
61, 63
Bhagat Singh Thind, 4–5, 6
bias: against African Americans, 39–40;
of church behavior, 69; race terms
and, 55
Bill Moyers Journal, 40
biracial: children, 15; *mulatto/quadroon/
Octoroon* terms for, 30

About the Author

Dr. Paul R. Lehman, who earned a Ph.D. from Lehigh University, 1976, is a university Professor Emeritus in the department of English, and a former Dean of the Graduate College, at the University of Central Oklahoma, Edmond, Oklahoma. He is married with two adult sons. His wife Marion is former elementary school teacher; his older son Christopher is a professor in Ethnic Studies. His youngest son Jeffrey is presently a high school band director.

His teaching experience spans a wide range of subjects including American Literature, Ethnic American Literature, Black American Literature, Short Stories, American Fiction, Contemporary Themes as Literature, and Chaucer.

Dr. Lehman has served on many state boards and councils including the Board of Trustees of the Oklahoma Connections, Oklahoma Foundation for the Humanities, Oklahoma Alliance for Arts Education, Oklahoma Folk life Council, Edmond Arts and Humanities Council, Let's Talk About It Oklahoma, Oklahoma Connections, and the Oklahoma State Regents for Higher Education Council for Professional Teaching Standards. He was also a former CBS (affiliate) News Anchor, Producer, and Reporter.

He has lectured throughout the state of Oklahoma as well as in other states across America. He has published scholarly books, scholarly and creative articles, poetry, short stories, interviews, books, and book reviews. Other recent publications are *The Development of a Black Psyche in the Works of John Oliver Killens,* and *The Making of the Negro in Early American Literature.* He is active in both academic and community service. He is also listed in Who's

Who Among Black Americans, Who's Who in American Education, and Who's Who Among American Teachers.

Contact Information:
Dr. Paul R. Lehman
1313 Briarwood Drive
Edmond, Oklahoma
(405) 341-8773
E-mail: plehman@ucok.edu
pmlehman@cox.net